An Anthem for the Dreaming Lost

Samuel Hurley

www.samuelhhurley.com

samuel.hurley samuel.hurley

An Anthem for the Dreaming Lost

ISBN: 978-1-0686777-1-7 (Paperback)
ISBN: 978-1-0686777-0-0 (Hardcover)

First printing edition 2024.

Samuel Hurley
Unit 139492,
PO Box 7169,
Poole,
BH15 9EL

www.samuelhhurley.com

Contents

IV
My Life Is a Small Room Overlooking Time

V
The Boy Who Never Fell

VI
The Comet Sweeper

VII
I've Held You in My Arms as the Thing That Time Wants

VIII
Tomorrow - Forever

IX
Daphne

Preface

There is no set path ahead — you can make your way through this book from start to finish — you can pick at the poems over hours, weeks, years — lifetimes — you can read it backwards, upside down, sidewards — there are no rules past this point.

The poetry is split into chapters — some grouped by theme or time — others fragmented — existing as they should in their own little rooms, constrained to the moment they were formed. Some pieces are highly lyrical, some — plainly written — some will need no further investigation — their meaning being as obvious as a duck in a bowl of soup — others might require a second, third, even fourth read.

Whatever you gain from them — whatever you find; reflection — despair — beauty — boredom — frustration or exultation — you are correct. That is the beauty of poetry, it belongs to you, the reader — whatever you discover is a truth — a truth that is yours alone.

There is a hope — however — that along the way, you begin to see the fragments — the rough grains of a philosophy. One that stands against the disenchantment of our time — that rallies for the hidden beauty, the invisible moment — the joy of imagination, wonder and romance. Of being soft and naive — brave and magnificent — bold and authentic — in the face of a world that sometimes — often — almost always — is difficult to make sense of. That to live, to wake, to breathe and stand against the tide of all the troubles and grief we face and will come to face in life — is a victory. And to exist — an extraordinary gift.

I am ready,

here I stand —

come,
life, have me —
love me, like the
child who harms
the flower it wants
to know

An Anthem for the Dreaming Lost

We are not meant
to be this way,
to feel and not
come to feeling.

To have
sightless sight,
to pass beauty,
or to waste
in the maze
of night afraid
and dazed
of all tomorrows

To think that
the bright
in you was
just a light —

gone —

on that sexed
path through
a greased
teenage graceland —

or that growing
means to live
unmoved —
to come to
astonishment
without being
astonished

We are meant to
remember
our nature —

we are not meant
to forget that this

will not last —

that there will
be a final hour
a last time to
hold a hand
or look glad
upon the flower
to work from
your labyrinth
that book,
or to cook for
your mum

To kneel
before new
love and say
take my head —
or to waste
in some
earthy nook
a summer with
wine and sex

To not be timid,
or submit —

but to commit fully

It is not space,
nor time —

it is intimacy
that is the
last frontier
of our generation —

we have lost
our bravery

to be harmed
or come to
seeing harm
as the mark
of life —

that a suffered
thing has lived —

to know, to gamble,
to risk and dare
to be un-peeled
and yield to
the un-known…

To look
outward-in
and see —
that you are
not a thing
of fear
you are not a
spec alone —

you are the
un-parted pip
you are the grail
left by some muddy
fire in the first
flame of the
first red day
and it is
not yet out

It is always
too late to stray

but never
late enough
to say —

I am ready

Here I stand —

come,
life, have me —

love me, like the
child who harms
the flower it wants
to know

I

As a Boy I Stood Before a Tree

As a Boy I Stood Before a Tree

I

Six years old — I am shy — built like a secret — always
looking for the music of a quiet room — or the shadowed
sympathy of a corner — somewhere to stow my voice —

I covet the soft language of animals and the earth — my best
friend is a rabbit — Honey — our dialect is wordless —
bright

At night when it rains — I sneak past my brother's beds and
sit on the window sill — watch stray cats zip like salt-comets
under cars — singe orange under streetlight — press my
palm against the cool glass and the sorrow of the air —

everything is rhythmically sad —

some nights I steal downstairs and into the garden — take
Honey from her hutch — fall asleep as she chews through
wires — wake to angry parents and a flickering house

II

Honey is sick — she hides her body in the hay — she has
long shallow breaths — she refuses the carrots I give —

Dad says she is dying — that she is old — he's wrong —
friends don't die — yesterday she sat on my lap for an hour
— Dad asks if I want to say goodbye —

I slam the door — I hide in my room —

night comes — there are no stray cats — just bent, kind,
night — I look down to the hutch — in the morning she
will be okay

III

In the morning the hutch is empty — Dad says he is sorry — I ask where she is — he points to a box on the mantle — he asks if I want to see her one last time — I shake my head — he leaves the room — I stand in silence — I wait till I hear my father go upstairs — I grab the box and my bike — I zoom out of the house and into the woods — I skid and sit beneath a tree — I breathe — I wait — I hold the tragedy of the moment in the pearl of my throat — when I lift the lid — Honey will peer out, hop onto my lap — run about the field — she will be free — I shake — lungs vibrate — I open the box —

death is for movies and video games — death is pretend — death is Sonic falling off a ledge and coming back to the start — death is for old people — for relatives who never visit — death is for vampires and Goosebumps — death is a show — a theatre — a play — it's squinting your eyes and lolling out your tongue in a game of war — death doesn't come for rabbits — for friends — for the things a child loves

IV

We bury her in the woods — Dad says a few words — there's the green static of the river somewhere through the tree — the rusty smell of a barbecue in the air — I can't find anything in my head to say

V

Weeks pass — the summer holidays come — no school — the garden is quiet — its cracked tiles like a puzzle — the rain makes a soft buzz when it falls — like its falling in a cup — there's a mangled sorrow to my head — the hutch is gone — there's yellow-sour grass where it was — there's a silent clasp across life — it squeezes everything

VI

Dad takes my brothers and I out for a walk down to the woods — he tells us he has a surprise — a secret — he's found something —

we stop ten minutes down the path at the foot of a dead tree — crisp packets tackle nettle — there's a green gate twenty foot behind with a recently burnt sofa leant against the metal — in the distance there's the muffled sound of a marriage breaking —

Dad gets to his knees — gathers his boys around him — his usual theatrics — he talks about the legend of three faeries that live in these woods — in this dead tree — he points to a six inch arch — a hollow gash in the trunk —

he says we should write to them — that they still live there — that if we write they'll write us back —

my older brother asks what to write — Dad says anything — that they know everything — *they're magic* —

my brother's excitement is electric — I am silent

VII

My brothers write long mis-spelt passages — they scrawl — I sit for hours — ashamed of the muddy nut my brain is — the words are jumbled — tangled in abstracts — specs and rushes of feelings too large for the throat —

I write — *I'm sorry, Honey* —

I scrunch the paper into my pocket — strangling it like a neck

VIII

We each stand before the tree — my eldest brother places his letter in first — then my younger brother, Tom —

I step forward and pull the crinkled paper from my pocket — chuck it through the gap like a cloud into the night

IX

A few days pass — we wait around the hollow trunk as Dad reaches inside — he pulls out a palm of tiny envelopes — one for my eldest brother — one for Tom —

one for me — I hold it in my hand like holy parchment —

the faerie wrote back

X

There's a dull clunk of golf ball hitting club in the distance — they make little streaks in the sky as their plastic bodies kerb sunlight — down by the river there's a group of older boys chucking bottles into the water — they make a burbled pop — like the plug being lifted from bathwater —

we sit at the top of a bank — above the residence of endless nettle and bramble —

I look at the impossibly small writing on the white paper —

my eyes are swill with wet hope — my heart thumps like a rabbits foot --

the words are simple — astonishing —

Don't be sorry — Honey had three carrots this morning — she's happy — she misses you — how old are you Sam?

— *Six,* I say

— to myself — to sorrow — to the broken heart — to the trapped language of my head — to imagination — to the bridge of brightening that has opened up — to thunder — to the rain — to the white eyed poppet of the night — to the lonely hedgehog — the stray cat — the broken bottle — the burnt couch —

to the little faerie in a tree —

I'm Six

Another Poem on the Moon

I was seven — you millions of years young

You — grizzling light and
yellowing the garden with steep dreaming

Me — learning to draught my heart,
always leaning toward a window.

You — gelatinous and gleaming,
picking my brain like a tooth.
Saying it's all ache from here kid —
it's all longing and want
and spreading and trying
to spread. And hearing
music when you want to sleep
and sleeping when you want
to love — it's all creeping and
trying to unfold shade from the
packet of something brighter,
it's all thin tongue
starving for the name of spirit.
it's all rib trying to share
gas with woman —

Me — Whose words are these?

You — Ours

Me — How old am I?

You — Ancient. How old am I?

Me — Seven

Ego in an Orange Field

Alder — pine — heather,
they clan together to
suck the sticky-animus of
ego from thin walls
of the lung —

sublime earth —
its old mouth
on the naked
foot drives its
natural passengers
to the brain —

the body
is just mineral that
can feed the flowered
families of the earth

The self is a blazon
clot — the golden
tumour of Dream

Germ of My Brain

I skip college — dash cobble
in counterfeit Kickers — I pull
shadows from cigarettes, blow
blame from my mouth —

I wound worry with stolen
bottles of Lamb's Navy Rum —

when the pubs close I take the
long route back through the
wood — into its drunk darkness
— its blank paradise — its curly
shadows — its feminine horror
—

I sit in the hip of a tree full of
scratch — pricking the nights
black chase with the cherry of a
hot smoke —

I dig lyrics in my head — ornate
my lazy skull with rhyme and
liquid meaning —

I feel holy — divine and useless
— as though I can shrink to the
pinch of an atom — or in some
sweet bleak gain the blest privacy
ghosts have —

I feel close to something — a
high-beauty that can never be
electronic — that will always be
bloody and good and filthy —
that will always mine — because
it is — that rotten-golden-germ
of my brain — poetry

I Find Something Lovely in the Pond

I am often at the pond,
weed-throated;

its stench of magic,
the littered burble of its
lime-skin,
the hallowed shadow
of its pike — is a gift

its depth a green eye
with the mood of fortunes

I can pull poems here
from its everlasting sob —

dredge letters from its
nymphic soul
and give names
to sorrows I've had
— have

it reminds me I
was born like this
from its thick gob,

a dirty child —

grown out
into a mucky,
lovely world
that wants to be
undressed

Tilting a Neck Beneath the Sun

I have wondered how others see —

how alarmed they are by ruin,
or the prism above a breach;

light unions with water,
either by chaos or pattern,
furnishing some ancient skill,

and the eye invites or catches.

I have wondered how others see —

how easy they pass beyond this point,
that I so often stop at,
seeing vision in the bark;

terror woven in the beech,
a hundred faces screaming,
desiring to be out.

Or the gladness of Galilei
marking comets in the grain

It depends on a mood,
or the way sun falls

Astonish Me Muddy Thing

She says the boy must be muddy,

must know he's an insect,
be of the pond and hedgerow,
see night's waist and scrap
and never trim his sorrows and
he must come with his solace cut
and let me be it freely —
he must burrow it to mine
and have his mending body mend ours —

He must know it all hurts as it should
And that the hurt is truth.

Yes —

And that my brain is a teeming nature too,
full of riot and philosophy;
for I am the flower and the stave,
the lightning and the tremble
that I am rock and pip
and every gasping seed.

I am the choke and will
of one more day in the
sky of a dying thing —

and that I must — astonish

astonish — yes — I must astonish him.

I say — I am, you do.

13

Thirteen —

summer is open
like the guts of a pink fruit
there's a weeping flavour
everywhere;

citrine, peach — a young
musk to the water

I notice textures: cottons,
satins, the warmed orange
of a plastic chair

girls move — flock—colour
— I have epiphanies; Lily you are
a flower, Melody a song

Life is a slow-cinema
everyone is silver and faraway

My nose is doggish, it
can split the elements
of perfumes to its note,
or to the class
of the girl whose
nape it sweets

I obsess on geometry;
curves, curls,
the beveled shadows
in a blouse — the
shadowed corner
between english
and history

I look at my own life
through a pin

I need new clothes
new hair,

I want this old
head off my shoulders

I want to be lovely too

That Great Wizard the Bumblebee

Should I return to childhood
and sit by my childhood bed

I would say,

you are right, those poems
you wrote on the fridge are truths —

That the great wizard
is the bumble bee
and a mighty prophet too

Cats do dream
and seem to know
your thoughts - they do

That there is ever-beauty
always - but not always
plain in sight,
and that the sorrows in the darkness
are just the magicness of night.

That it is hard to bear a dream,
but harder to let one go
and it's through the art of suffering
that a dreamer's stuff will sow…

I might not say, that Tom,

our sweet Tom,
won't be on earth for long

But you'll see him once
again, when you hold your first born son.

And the voice you heard that night
was him calling all along.

I would say, you will
always be a big brother…

I would say stay, remain,
home is hard to find again
and it's lonely looking out at time
if you fail to foster friends…

I would say play,

stay out in the rain
kick the kerb, puck a penny,
make a den, scuff your knee,
hold your mother whilst she's young.

And write your poems,
they are truths -

I would say
there are
many happy days
but none as long as this.

But there is always wonder
If you remain true —

so do not, be stoic.

Do not be dream-proof.
Do not be dream-proof.
Do not be dream-proof,

I Am Unlike Paradise

I don't remember the words I said,

just your eye;

silent blasts of olive and amber peace.
pools of cell and glass — the fray —
the light-scare, the stay —

the homing shadow shone.

I was there — lay in the rye unfolding,
deforming in the heat

all; mass, protein and line,
gross and boyish and square

(I am so unlike paradise)

(so unlike how Michelangelo said)

But I was there — bred and
drossed in skin

Is that me?

Did a thing ever speak my name,
or know of me till now?

Time's Minstrel Tell

The child plucks buttercup,
its gold-death follows her home

She hasn't the ear to hear
it is the mirror of time's minstrel tell

The sorrowed sympathy that is
the happy pluck of her own skull
from its own sweet shell

But it is that memory;

the flower from its palaced
cell that calms the soured
miniature of life's last breath

(the charm of time's
told symmetry)

and at her death
she will say —

yes now I see

that that hour
this earth
that flower
that life
— was me

I Should Stray

I already decay,

if I tightly close my eyes
I see the particles away,
drifting from my skin,
raving in the dark

I already wane;

in day I see the contour
of my shadow strain
peeling life off
skin's brief pool

So I should stray,

and not go this same road

I Return Home Bloodied

I do not know how to un-crease
(how to be at ease)

nor to un-desire —
to remain these feet still,
when thinking of the Pennines
or the blood you hush —

or writing for the rose mallow
that could have journeyed the dune,
or writing for the wanderer
for the waster and the lost —

or the sorrow that rushes
when I think of Manderley

I do not know how man neatens.

How he remains at home un-bloodied.

How he returns in — unscathed —
unmoved by petal, throat, breast.

How he stays un-fascinated,
how he does not tangle
into every common thing
and live its pain

How he does not say,

yes — bleed me too.

Seeing Through the Mountain

Everything has yield,
something tinted
in its width or depth

the mountain with
its steep beauty
submits to the
painter and the
mountaineer alike

Through eye
Through sinew

it makes the living
wait and wants its
admirer to seduce
or attack in foreplays
of pick or pen

its very stoned neck is
open to address — to the violent
tenderness of being had
— being known

of saying

there is a million years
of secrets in my body

like you

like us

Summary of a Future Death

I wrote, I leaned to this.

Day: I stood beyond that tree,
and caught its grazing shadow,
and like my father said,
reared its shape to page,
and took its render home to you.

Night: I stayed and lived with
light and read, and played and
rarely slept. And I always told
the airy heat what I most wanted
and you said I didn't need to
believe in heaven —
I never told you if I did.

Morning: I strayed and never lived
like the crowd or did as
I was taught to do and I loved
and lay as I was warned against,
and gave all my rushes to it.

And night again: I listened and listened
and then I spoke and gave
the lost things their voice.

I wrote, I did lean to it

Yet nothing ever went my way,
and it was ugly like you warned,
but beautiful like I knew it would be.

Dual Sight

Our first brain is the
the natural creature — a poet

it curls in the skull with its drooped doom
and fascination — the world to it is legend —

in childhood it has full reign of
sensuous power — it covets the mineral
energy of fantasy — it sucks the heaving
spirit of each item to the eye — it builds
ghosts and little gods — it feels the
murder of the night — it feels
the shadow's sympathy too —

in teenage years it has its last fevers —
as the second brain comes through —

it strikes hormone — cakes it
with sexual symmetry and
eternities of youths violet —
it gives it seven more years of talent —
but causes harm to its host as
its fantasies fail proof —

the second brain is reason —

it has lighted enlightenment — it
thins by measure the shadowed
flesh of first creation — by
measure it limits a depth — it
brings to wonder's sulking cot
its law and map — it has wins —
things of function — triumphs and
successes in material — solid life --

the monied world has no purse for
fancy — no application
for astonishment —
or value in the mythic head —

so the poet sleeps — and the adult toils —
and the poet's eye is dead —

and the adult can't find meaning —
forgets his childlike joy — the
beating pulse of life, ebbs
and dries to bored machinery —

till — in some depression —
or sickness — or in a lover's
mad spell — he senses the
first head's — first magic skill —
and through reasoned eases —
he lets between the metric
eves — art's magic consciousness —

then begins the curdling of a light —

to look on life — twice — as child and
adult — lamb and tyger

The Recurring Dream

I

Time is cyclic —

it tells its truth
through small magics,

its show is a ritual
that sometimes repeats
or comes as a singular graphic;

- *The recurring dream*
- *A rare moment that wounds belief*

Its art is to misbelieve
Its proof is proofed-future
It has the comic of hindsight
at its lead

II

From age seven to ten I had a repeating dream;

I sit under the stairs and lift the receiver of the house phone. On the other end there's two voices. One I recognise as mine, the other I cannot place. But I know it is my brother. We are saying goodbye to each other. I weep. It is a goodbye forever. I listen to myself beg him to stay. He cannot. The voicemail ends. I wake.

I cry. And cry. And cry.

III

My brothers are alive. We dance to our parents music — Buddy Holly, Queen, The Beatles… we hop round our small bedroom rocking our necks like Egyptians to the Bangles.

I'm the middle child. I have the privilege of being big and small — in-between

Childhood speeds — its scuffed knees, its frogs and newts, its sleepovers. We scar the house, make dimples in the walls, write secrets on the peeling wallpaper.

My brother's are alive.

IV

I ask my mother if there was a fourth. A phantom child. Someone secret.

No.

There was only ever three.

V

I'm Eighteen.

I have the dream one last time. I keep it to myself — there's a comfort in it, something knowing, something that feels part of who I am— it's a thread to my childhood, something golden and sad — just fiction.

I read about twins that in the womb dissolve the other. I think maybe the dream is an echo, some melded psyche, the residue of a second life I might have had.

Life zooms ——————

I move on,

I dive into rivers, I swoon — I turn emo and punk and lash out and last until the sunrise with all the birds and drunks. I write poems and poems and poems. I make plans and wild futures.

I'm still a middle child. My brothers are alive.

VI

I'm Twenty Three. October 12th.

There is a strangeness to that night. I change my plans. I cannot settle. I cannot eat.

I head out with a friend into town. I have an overwhelming feeling that I need to see my younger brother, Tom, who is out with friends at a local pub. I ask the taxi to divert —

And there he is — my little brother — my best friend. Little Thomas; born with three holes in his heart, with punctured lungs, with scoliosis so bad he never grew past five foot. My little brother; with all his challenges, the hospital stays, the surgeries. The little brother I worried about being bullied, or attacked. The little brother I took shopping before he went to university so he could have some *cool* clothes. The little brother who only a month ago I had to rescue from his student flat because a party had got out of hand — stands amongst his friends, the life of the party, the joy of the pub.

He's funny. Swill with light and laughter. Everyone wants to talk to him.

We share stories, I ask him what he wants for his birthday next week.

I lend him a tenner.

But we have to go — my friend says we've stayed too long.

I hug Tom, we say we love each other.

VII

I don't stay out long. The music was off. The beer wasn't right. I leave on my own and return home. It's midnight. I can't sleep. I stay up, writing, watching old movies, I sit on the window ledge and watch the cats. I smoke.

My mother calls.

"You need to get to the hospital."

"What's wrong?"

"It's Tom… he's collapsed…"

Tom's collapsed before. I throw on my coat and call a taxi. It will be okay. He will be okay.

"He'll be okay?"

My mother's voice falters.

"I don't think so Sam."

VIII

October 13th. 3am. Stepping Hill Hospital.

Mum waits in the adjacent room. A nurse comes in. They say the doctors are working on you. That they are trying their best.

Tom. There are four doctors, nurses, surgeons. I don't know who or what they are. But they press on your chest. You look sweetly asleep, there is a blue skim to your lip — your eyes are shut in some nearby dream. I remember you being smaller — in primary school you were so small you'd run through the middle of adult's legs. I remember you coming back from a hospital stay when you were six, and standing in assembly as everyone clapped and cheered because you were back. I remember the joke you told everyone a million times that week - what do you call a donkey with three legs? — A wonkey. I remember just last year walking through Topshop with you, helping you choose a jacket. Last week I came home early so I could sit and watch Supernatural with you. We talked about your movie script. I shared some poems. We made plans to move out together.

I hold your cold hand. I try and will these memories to you.

I don't know what to say. I'm full of fear. Full of anger. Full of pain.

I beg you to stay. To fight. To wake. I scream that you aren't supposed to leave me. You aren't allowed to. In Supernatural, brothers Sam and Dean always stick and stay together. They never give up. I say it's your birthday in two weeks. I tell you, you promised we'd move out together. That we're supposed to do life together — to face it all, become great writers.

I tell you I'm sorry. That you are my little brother. That maybe I could have saved you.

I hope you heard me.

I meant it all.

I hope you know how much I loved you — love you.

IX

October 13th 4am.

The light goes out.

X

A dream — many years later
I sit under the stairs and lift the receiver of the house phone. On the other end there's two voices. One I recognise as mine, the other is my brother Tom's. We are saying goodbye to each other. He tells me not to weep. He is safe, he says — it is not goodbye forever. We will see each other again.

XI

2020. October 13th. 4am. Stepping Hill Hospital.

My first son is born — he is light and fresh and hot pink. He is healthy and loud and screams with the wild voice of new life.

He is bright like you, Tom.

XII

Time is cyclic —

it tells its truth
through small magics,

its show is a ritual
that sometimes repeats
or comes as a singular graphic;

- *The recurring dream*
- *A rare moment that wounds belief*

II

Every Name You’ve Ever Had

Every Name You've Ever Had

This is remembering I've known
every name you've ever had,

how you appear like moss;
cut-angel — autumn's flush
or like the long-knife of winter
or white when the powers out.

This is remembering
that you were leaf

That you were gossamer
pine and gore,
this is remembering
that you were once an
atom in some drunk
shepherd's sleep

Once the mineral
in the mountains teeth
the gaoler in the dirt
beneath Sca Fell -
the gloaming
by the heath.

That I was once Precambrian dew
waiting for the sun
to dry my skate
or for a cirrus in which to roost
so I could come home
and love you

again

Your Architect Was a Dreamer

Your architect was a dreamer —

must've been.

You are florescent in the dark
of this house

There's not been a night
since we met

There is too much of you
made from light that
even sleep dreams.

To close my eyes is
not to shut but to wake —

To break any hour of
sadness I only need to blink.

Yes.

There you are.

You spill when laying,
flowing over sheet,
emerging as a pattern.

An early sequence
designed to stray.

Who made you?

I could write a book
on beauty with
just your name.

Like Breath

I write you with difficulty,

if you knew how you
sounded as I look —
you are loud to the eye;

life is an anthem of suns,
there is heat to
the thoughts of you,

the clock taints,
your body flatters time,
it moves your shadow
on the desk —

It is religious
to know you,
there's a hymn to
who you are,

to have you lay
across the mind.

I sleep awake;

Nights are the
glass of churches,
life looks through
seeking at you.

Everything I stem
is low-bright,
never peaching,
never right

But there might be
simple words
for you —

like life — maybe breath.

Human Sorrow

To love is to know human
sorrow. The eye panics in front
of loveliness — the ego wilts,
the mouth fails too — it starves
for comparison. You begin
to promise things you do not
have — stars, planets, forevers.
It is the comic tragedy of life
that immortal love is given to
the mortal host. That in some
bloodied rush, you feel the
flame of something infinite but
understand that nothing lasts.

This Isn't Our Lifetime

It is the
same pleasure;

apple-skin sun,
the piled wave
the fell of Haworth
to the reader's head
the tucked mist
over Gragareth
as it curds new myth —

as it is to know
you — to know you exist.

It is the
same pain;

the untouched lip
the empty hand
the Gorgon's bed
the hare beneath
the hawk in
the emerald of
Eave's Wood —

to know you
have to go,

to know it does
no good

to know that this
isn't our lifetime love

Love & Sorrow

I have these bones — ***take them***

Before I cast them in the earth
and make the angels of you in soil

Or have this poem, it too is like dirt
it has grown and lost you

Have this atom — this scan of me
in light

But let me keep this brain —
it has an image of you today - forever

Let it sleep

Let it have great heavy dreams
that bends skins
and makes of men new things

It might wake some night
and speak —

Where are you?

I would take
anything you give,

I would marry myself to your whisper,
or to the gravity on your pillow

It is the last piece of all
the sorrows —

No

Not sorrow — ***love***.
But, they're the same aren't they?

Sleep Re-Paints You

Your face seems always new,

Morning sees soft gradation —
a reveal of unknown line.

With her stray,
sun admits new freckle,
where yesterday
we lay in grass.

Lips blush and pale,
nursing shadow —
keeping secrets in.

Wine has groomed
away a white,
and lit greenness
in your eye.

(So now I am confused of colour.)

Even as I re-write this, your
beauty changes as you wake.

Sleep re-paints you.

Our Love Is a Muscle

Our love is a muscle
that lasts forever —
we shall not be laid to rest

These bodies are brief nests

Our bloods may string — our calcium zest
and live in the bright heads of buttercup —

but we will stay

The future was yesterday

The earth has been our statue
it will till us till it breaks

That little sorrow — to lose our breath,
or lament the mess that death makes —

Do not mind it

It is dark matter that
tucks us — binds us in

My eyes find beauty
where it steeps

I have sleep that
finds you anywhere —

we cannot be lost

Let Our Bodies Write

I want new language,
something like the
earth speaks

I want the words
the river writ
I want the tones
stones make
against the beach

I want to breach
light — borrow
her mouth

I've seen how she
takes trees

They are changed
after —
they have
poems that last planets

I think it's in us

that chord
that Cohen wrote

It is the photon
between touch
it is the sing
that teeth teach

Now there's a music

I hear it —

We should sweat it off,
let it write

The Relic of a Lonely Night

Hello night —

your face is famous to me,

I was a boy dreaming of your black halls
of the bodies in your pale house

I was afraid, too fresh faced
for sorrow.

I was late.
I said things.

But that was then

I've lived the harm men live
and now, there's a woman —

She has the foster
of your touch

— there is wines silver to her hips.
she lives my hours darkly,

There are quarries that through her
find my secrets

She is a beauty as gentle as violence

But I was just a child
when I wrote that hymn

I was scared of the dark.

But it is, isn't it? It's her.

On the Colour of Her Eyes

Whilst framing
your iris

I have drawn
out all light
from the corners
of this house.

Have;

laid new paint
upon the wall,
glossed the capture
of a shadow,
and blessed
it twice —

have;

drawn all
light back,
invited gleaming
to its hovel,
and addressed
this colour twice;

they look
like this —

a ring of greening
mourning blue,
then night
spooks the hue,
and light with
its high array
pans peace of
amber from
them too

I do not know
their colour

they have
the pleasure
of atmosphere,
they amend
with nature's
mood —

it takes a poem
to tell the truth.

Our Normal Paradise

Then if there is
no heaven,

nor voice,
nor Valhalla
on which to rest,

then if I can not live
again and return home
to you in happiness,

then have these words,
whilst I have breath;

I am thankful
I found you

Someone to share in loveliness,

to double the wins I had,
to half the crown of loss
and light the split of loneliness.

And in that flash — that
cinema of life's last sight

It will not be some holy summer,
nor alarm, nor sonic ministry

— it would be this slight love,
this common bless
I see before my death;

Our tedious day,
the gallery of our laugh,
red wine in the bath,
the torn winter coat
the misspelt note
on the fridge —

It will be these triumphs
that go with me in the light

It will be this normal, boring
lovely little life we had,

that I miss,

that I hold,

that I take,

that goes out —

into the dream of that long night.

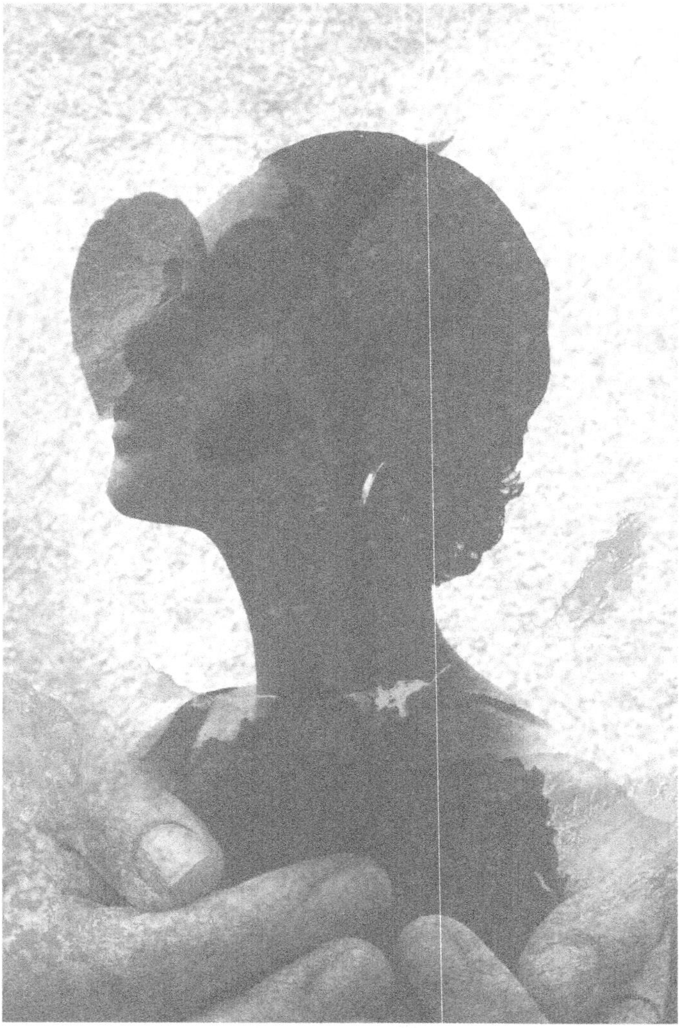

III

You Are Still That Tiny Atom

There Is Wonder

And maybe you'll forget sometimes,

and in forgetting come to hate your skin,
or feel your passion cede
and mind-side the sun will dim,
rid its grains of amber,
the inward eye will slim,
and see not a patch of heaven,
and in your search for meaning,
you will find the meaningless in things.

But there is — ***wonder.***

not back-turned or stoic,
or bid for someone else
but onward calling ever —

there, on the cradle of chestnut net with fire
in tinnitus, in tv-static or a fairy horn blown from Gower,
or it's there in the lonely hour
where sorrow is waste and vast,
and yet, some lost song, or faded floral
dress, or in the hallow crevice of your slanted childhood bed,
or hivey-scent of baking bread,
brings the bone back without body and
learns the spirit out -

yes spirit —

lean to it,
phase your eyes so
it can onward seek the
magic of a thing —
the inside life of life
and you might remember
what you are.

And in remembering know
Avalon or Blake's Jerusalem

or hear the names of insects on
the television.
and again love the flower
and understanding then that in
the simple power of a thought
the world was born.

And in this you will see yourself
and in seeing know, and knowing love
the thing you are —

just a flash in a skull full of worship,
a dream not yet burnt out.

Be Tender

I am often left here bleeding.

yet cannot close my heart,
nor glance away its nature;

ignore the ruins of a life,
or the royal-ness of being.

Too long is the ache, to be uncaring —
a pale road lined with window;

experience knocks, beauty haunts,
new faces arrive and it is
un-known if they are faithful —

risk.

To be tender is an agony,
and often I am bleeding,
but my heart goes ready on gazing

I will not shut it — nor should you

A Greater Romance

I could fall away
from this thesis into practice,

could;

proffer saddening from its still,
and pursue the 'Great Romance'
the concealed nature of a thing,
and its magnificence.

I could away — away and write
these details as I see them,
loan my body to a roaming
that leads the long alone,

to a knowing no one knew before
and remain myself.

I could leave this room, this bed,
this hour —

I could away — away and disband
the components of my figure,
leaving my histories on scraps of paper —

my legs, my eyes, my hands
etc…

My Hands Were Once Green Too

Say Earth my hands were once green too

they held Pritt stick and ash,
a recipe for Welsh rarebit. And
a prayer. I'm nine, there is
semolina on my top,
I do not know we are
poor, and I do not that this is happy.

This is knowing
I hold too much empty space,

this is remembering
in sleep I am born from peat
and not from mother at all —

and I am like you,
and swell and die,
and on repeat

And there is nothing
under my brain,
because I glad it out

and I don't dream-in-dream
of sky or angel,
I'm just one long vein,
in a dancer on and on.

I am greeny and un-shy,
I am a boy full of earth
with no room for heaven.

Childhood Relics

Childhood relics hold magic —
they are saturated with the hours
you spent brightly at their hem,

the doll — the toy car — the
mothed teddy — the songs
and rhymes —

remain enchanted —

in their skins — their
melodies or ancient
crayon —

are shed-soul —

doorways to
the splintered self

these are things you once
loved — felt loved by once,

turn on that old show — the
match you watched with
your dad — the music you
danced to with your mum —

you will see that you are
not lost — you are yet not
done with the dream
you once had

Victory! Human Thing

Oh human thing, there is no light in
being a machine

It is not the hour to upgrade or
allow yourself to be replaced

nor to be chased from your rightful
place on this blithe planet

It is not your victory
to live forever,

or to trade your skin
for some electric dream —

yours is the cosmic gene —

You are Nature's witness
to time's comic paradise

Human thing your
victory is music,

it is the poem,
it is the branched
air between a kiss,
the held hand,
the triumph
of an ordinary day,

it is the sensuous
mortal task
to hunt life's
perfumed hiss,

or to the spend
the normal
miracle in your
head and add it
to the human sum.

The human story
is not yet done.

It is not time
to be post-human,
it is time to be
most human.

No living thing
at the arcades of death,
prays for more profit,
more metal a better job,

they want for breath,
for a last embrace,
in their final vision
it is in the visit of their
mother's human face,
or some sweet friend
or mortal joy that sends
them on their way —

there might come
a time when we
say we are done with
human things —

but it is
not this day.

Today is for
human victory —
human thing.

And I can promise you this —
if a digital thing had a wish,
it'd wish for this;

This painful, beautiful,
strange and comically brief
trial of life,

It would want for the air,
for the sun, for grass,
for the touch of rain
on a plain and human face

It would trade its immortal place
for a brief childhood of skin —

for the grace that comes from love —
with all its troubles and bliss.

It would surrender everything

for your life,

for your pain

for your triumphs

for your human victory —

the victory to live.

To exist.

Epiphany

Epiphany;

it is a streetlight as it drips,
splashing memory
of somewhere else

It is following the glum
gem from a cigarette
to the female lines
drawn by snow,
and seeing Asra,
or any un-gainable
love between
shock walls of ice

And saying yes,
and letting the heavy
brain be heavy

And letting the tired
heart tire

And letting the broken
shatter

- saying mend or no,
I do not mind

I do not dislike who
I am anymore

Glad

I am glad I forget things — that
sometimes I am late —sometimes
break or shatter —that
sometimes I cannot cope or find
a way —

I am glad for hurt — I am glad
for these scars and this burning
grief —

I am glad I can scream — I am
glad that I am not glad that you
are gone — that it will never be
okay — I am glad I can miss you
— and torture myself with these
patterned memories —

I am glad I have no escape even
in a poem —

I am glad I keep the things I
should not keep —

That I will go into the greened
earth full of secret and unfinished
hopes —

I am glad even for this dirty
home — for the sofas you sat
on — for the marks my children
make on the wall — for the
damp that floats in its grey
abstract — that sometimes has a
humour — or the shape of places
we did not go —

I am glad even that some day I
will die and not want to die and
that in wanting to stay, I will be
glad of all the human life I had

This House of Lightning

Three years old, my son is a dash
— a pink streak — the world is
a first morning — its simplest
items astonish — everything has
worth — spills with meaning —
he holds common species like
rare delights — scoops of dirt as
though its tourmaline or jadeite
—

he whips over fields — clasps
fistfuls of dandelions and
clenches of grass — stuffs his
pockets full of pebbles — drops
them at his Mother's feet —
gives me yards of peculiar sticks
—

and I see — this is what love
is — bringing beauty back —
saying look — it's lovely and I
want you to see it — it's beautiful
— all of it —

he'd build us a home like this —
a house of lightning — made of
pebble and shock — a place light
lives — a habitat to remember
that the world was — still is —
wonderful — that maybe we just
forgot —

that's what love is isn't it?

Waking someone up

The Call

This is the call.

If you hear the flower say paint me.
Paint it.
If your pain says write me.
Write it.
If your loss says survive me.
Survive it.

And if your heart says do this because
it brings you joy — lean to it.

Listen.

And do it.

Do it if it doesn't pay.
Do it if it doesn't make you famous.
Do it if you think you're not good at it.
Do it if you're not the best.
Do it even if it hurts and if you have to do it alone,
Do it so you might not feel lonely.

Do it because you must.

This is the call.

To respond to the nature of your spirit.

And if you need, if these parts of you are lost,
in some maze of adulthood with all its rules
and trials, and drawing out —
go back to your childhood,
remember what brightness was in you.

And you'll see.

It remains.

And you'll see that is the call.

No matter how small you have come to

think your art or self is worth, to contribute

And you must contribute.

And I mean this, in all its terror and beauty —
So remember it.

The time you have is already ending.

So say something.
Do not go silently.

Tell Someone Who You Are

I

Mum waits outside the hospital — she stands forty foot away — her arms wrapped round her twelve year old coat — the worn navy spitting out bubbles of frayed cotton — she holds herself — cradles her body — soothes herself with the care her own mother once gave to her —

I wait — tucking breath into my lung — unable to move — trying to convince myself of absurdities — like — cancer is normal — that parents die — that miracles happen — that Mums live forever —

I suck in air — bite for its mineral courage — walk towards her — layer smile over worry — she reaches for me — hugs me like I might vanish —

II

It's humid — inside we wait for information — there's an anxious tropic — a sterile oxygen in the doctor's office — Mum grips my hand so tight bones overlap — the pain is good — we're alive — it clenches the moment — makes it important — bookmarks it —

time is different in hospitals — in the present it's languid — sinister — clock fingers shimmer over minutes — warble back and forth — collecting tiny echoes of breath —

they leave you in these horrible rooms — in minor eternities — sound collapses in — gathers in the drum of your ear — pools in your neck — forces confessions from the throat — conversations you wouldn't normally have —

I don't know why — but I ask Mum if she could go back and do anything differently — change a part of her life — live something new — what would it be —

she doesn't hesitate —

She says — I'd have been an actress —

there's the tremor of dreaming to her lip — a brave quiver — it's not a tragedy — it's a brightness — a peeling — she's not telling me who she might of been — she's telling me who she is —

My Mother — who has worked all her life as a psyche nurse — who has selflessly raised three boys on her own for the past fifteen years — who has never asked for anything — never wanted for herself — or demanded anything from life but a roof over her head and safety for her sons —

is an actress —

the door swings open — threatens to sweep the moment with its draught of panic — but I catch it — tuck it into my rib —

the doctor sits — murmurs through inertia with medical jargon — latin magics — mostly vapour through anxious heads — we wait for something we can grasp — something that sounds human — something triumphant —

the news is good — the surgery a success —

we gasp — want to stand and shout — want to hallelujah — but we rattle with little happy tears — pinch each other — indenting the moment — making it real — hoping it is —

III

On the way home — there's the feel of a future in the car — the whisk of time to the air — there's still work to be done — check ups — scans — there's a possibility it might come back — but for now — there is an endless hour to our words —

Mum gets out of the car — she walks into the house — I
wait in the driver's seat — take a second to myself — and
cry —

I pull the out the grain she gave me — the dreamed
confession — my mother is an actress —

though I hope she is the exception — the anomaly — the
mother who lives forever — who sits above time and
tomorrow — someday I will have to say goodbye — I will
have to speak in past tense — tell my sons who she was —

I'll say — she was an actress — and in my memories —
when dream brings her back — swarms her in the light —
I'll see her standing on a stage — as the icon she was — the
paradigm of love in the theatre of my life

You Are Still That Tiny Atom

No creature is designed to
hide from its own habitat —

to stowaway from its abode —

this earth — this blue rock —
its woods, its vales — its
rivers and seas — its mountains —
its deserts its fells and brooks
and pleasant lea's —

it is yours — it is ours
— our ancestral house.

You once loved this planet —
once felt loved by it —

once moved with it as it
formed, were kin and
skin in its wet mantle.

It is time — to say —

I am still that green
skinned child —

still the body in the reed,
still the wonder on the stone —

still the heart upon the rosses,
the skin beneath the bird —
the bone above the worm.

To say — I am still that tiny atom,

to say — I am human — I am back,

I am here — I am home

IV

My Life Is a Small Room Overlooking Time

Panic!

It's the eighth time I've been to the doctor's that month — the night before I lay awake staring at the ceiling — my eyebrows flickering and twitching — my brow lighted with a carnival of electric insect — I dug my nail into my cheek certain my whole head had gone numb —

the MRI I had was wrong — and the CAT scan — and the echocardiogram — and the blood tests — and the chest x-ray — and my glucose monitor —

when I walk — the world tumbles — my eyes look through soured lenses — everything is out of focus — unsettled — nervous — sometimes it gets too much and I hide under a table — sunglasses on — the light is a scar to my thoughts — it ruptures the complete pieces I once owned — I decay little particles where I sit — grasp at them to stay whole —

I've spent a year in the house — barely leaving — looking out of windows — googling diseases — I've had them all — I've grieved my life — said goodbyes each fortnight —

I'm alive somehow — though barely — I'm near death — can smell its putrid hand — its scorched glee on every bevelled glass — its coat in the sleek fringe of evening — under the grey pastures of furniture —

sleeping is tinted horror — barely a pause — I wake like being dropped into water — plunged from subconscious-solid into the frozen wet ego —

My GP looks at me with soft little eyes — I think it could be pity —

It's my head — I say — *maybe it's encephalitis* —

before I can say anymore — before I can pull the sheet of paper I've printed out — on symptoms — reactions — allergies — she breaches the space between us — takes my hand —

Sam — she says — *are you hearing voices?*

my eyes skin with water — there's a sad fruit in my throat
— there's a scream somewhere in its pip — rotten and old
— I'm scared — terrified of my own brain —

help — I've lost my head

Carousel

The dark gnat in the corner
of a good time — is death —

— we have held to each
other like orphans in a
flood — dug into youths
sexual symmetry — sucked
the dreams from each others
mouths — loved the germs
we make as our own creatures —

but death —

it is the silent parcel passed
between us — time —
nothing lasts —

no matter how much
we build this love — or
drive femur vs femur,

death will come —

tonight or in some future'd
sleep — and crack our skulls —
sip this romance and its host
from our molecular cup

Say —

you've had your fill,

back to the carcass —
to the carousel and
and into soil again

Apple

Kate — you are
that lovely
mouldering apple —

I am a worm
in the dying of
your bright organ

my house
is sweet
because
of memory

I am alive
because I
loved you.

The Head

The original nature
of the head
is the poem.

The eye was
meant to undress,

to skin happiness
from happy skin.

Everything's
beauty
is sad,

love is a blue
fire with
an unhappy ash.

You dust for years
and find its
celled pleasure
in your fingernails.

Jerusalem

Some summers I see dresses,
withering on a wire,
and fill them full of skin with my eye.

Make them amble from their
hanging and life them to a wonder —

to a rich disease,
well in suffering.

Sometimes,

(too often) I name flowers
after your other men,
and cut their stems.

Sometimes this teenage illness in me
appears ahead, screaming like
stone deforming from a church.

Sometimes I hear Jerusalem.

Sometimes I sing back.

A Poem Tries To Imitate

There's an ancient sweat
to the room — the human
memory of human movement

of thousands of footsteps;
the rubber scar
of trainer and boot
— the red scent
of burnt heel
of skin happily
away from skin

I sit in the corner —
two girls from class
dance latin,

they roll like wine,
they swarm with
a hot secret beneath
the cloth they wear,

it's easy for them —

as easy as I can make
a fist or make a manic
from a simple thought,

they glide with the
natural magnesium
of bone,
jewels of water in
their hair

I know in that
moment that
man is always at a window
— a witness to beauty

I know why a poem
is never finished

It wants to move like
this — it wants in

Surgery for the Ego

To the ego,

which is not always as you see it,
and often wants to kill its host
or abandon when its dream is low

It does show —

in moment — the
arrogant boon of hope
and gifts some brilliance

Yet a doubt will make it go

Often is it leading,
pleading on to write,
or to charge toward
the glory
of an angel in the night

Not an angel after all
just the dying of a light

Not a light after all
just the edge of something
bright

Not bright after
all just the muscle of
an animal looking
at time

Hi, Shadow

A seasoned shadow does not
dissipate at the edge and
can often be
confused with a door.

But this is false —

this type of shade is shut
and is only aesthetic in its purpose;

you cannot wrap it round your
fingers on a bridge of brightened sun,
nor create puppets on the wall
of your childhood bedroom —
and a flashlight has little use
at scattering its cut.

It may sometimes resemble a minor god
or the legacy of a once blooming garden,
(mine once looked like Eris)

but it is not.

It is a shadow — you cannot rid nor tame it.

I Might Forget

It is all vanishing,

the gore of daylight;

swallow spin, tumbling
skyward in a brake,

the rake of sun flecks
upon the last of wine,

hue blisters on the grape,
then sweeps its girls away.

Fawn, dithering, meek
retreat within the tree

to their mothers cautious tow.

What do they know?

In a gale — go,
it aways our flesh.

I fear sleep.

I might forget you.

A Ritual

I am often ripe with wonder —
full of eye.

Detail flushes, freckling,
spec undresses in its particle.

I can dwell in a moment
and live upon it,

just a fleck of brightening
elongates my day —

I am often on a road to beauty —

but can be struck down mightily
by a sorrow I knew was waiting,

or an absence I patched with invention.

And neither chemic nor music helps.

Then life seems a long grief —
a ritual before dying.

Melancholia

There is a sorrow
that seeks you,

it is in the
tumble of a bee
or the braise of
nettle on the shin,
or in the passing of the
window of a house
you once lived in.

It is there —
if you've known it,
in the early blood
of spring,
when the sprig and
lamb make their race
towards the sun —

or in the moon of
a memory of your
Mother's voice,

or in the question of
a child who looks at life
headwards on —

and asks — ***what are you?***

In the falter of that answer
is a sorrow that seeks you

It may come
to you tonight,
when your house has
no room to stow the
dreaming or the
tenets of your life —

then it it will come.

It may be winged
or have a face
or to it have
the chase of light
the patter of a
school yard rhyme
or is simply
just the silence
between the
tangles of your life —

but do not hush.
Stay it —
hold it close

there is all the
beauty in it,

it will bear you softly
on your course,
and let you know
you are not done —

it will tell you
who you were

it will show you
what you might
become — tomorrow.

For you are not done.

Lodark

I am sometimes slow to sleep,
too tangled in philosophy.

I am sometimes too fast at dreaming,
too quick to pocket beauty,
that is in the morning gone.

Sometimes I steal the silence
you make between a breath,
and write a line upon it.

— sometimes I hate myself.

Sometimes I steal the silence
you make between a breath,
and write a lie upon it

— often I hate myself.

I am sometimes slow to sleep,
and the night is loud
and has an anthem of memory
to whittle it —

sometimes I want to wake you.

But what would I say?

I Was That Green Headed Boy

And I must say this before I sleep —

— the pall may slip.
and you may miss me,
and find the narrow light lighten.

And say he never was
that glistening boy
nor silver lipped nor
quick to wit

and never was
a bright thing bright
or hot with meaning —

no, never was there meaning
or a gleaming to be found

But, there was.
I was.

Is.
Am.

On Swallowing Your Loveliness

I am demented by love —

I wash the skin of you
with the normal lyrics
of the earth

My teeth are crickets
in a wood,

that is a bird — this is a bird

Your dress hits the ground,
your bra over your head,
our shadows are hushed
animals hunting music

I call the odours of night
perfumes —

I call myself a creature

I say my heart is half
a gendered stone

On evenings I listen
sadly to happiness
when you're gone

I forget happiness
I forgo it

I hold my neck
and its white
flesh
to keep your
loveliness in

Upon a Gutter Staring

I am like all vanishing things —
Taraxum — van de graaf.
I am like the great vanishing things —
Engravings — Galilea.

As the famed vanishing things —
Wealth — love — super 8.
Lipstick as it dissipates,
Or as it looses mouths parting.

Tongue as it guides voice,
Or looms between hips,
Lettering notes.

Like grand vanishing things —
Light — Motes.

I am like all vanishing things,
Poltergeists — the lost.

Here — Away.

Am I sometimes strange to touch?
Am I sometimes difficult to love?

I think I am.

Dive Into Something Sacred

Thousands under roof;
in love and dying —
they worry then cease,
passing their grieving
onto children.

Others wrinkle
tomorrows with
the long ache of debt.

Many squander beauty,
and sell their sense to
electronics —

Forgetting the smell of rain,
or the simple grace of body
without cosmetic,

or the elegant state of
sex and love (combined).

Most languish on a dream,
and feed it as their
hours ruin.

Few step outwards
into fear and live.

Love Is a Futurist

Some harm hides itself,
(in art — sex— song)

It has to be brought to
you in abstract;

A minor chord,
the image of a mother
on the stone,
Ophelia — Millais,
a tongue passing
through the lip

It is why beauty
seems to ruin
— it knows our hope

Love is a futurist,
it scans childhood

It says tomorrow
we may fill,
we might heal,

having not remembered
we were cut

Let Me Decay in This Green State

I could linger here;

flaking blossom sailing down
with the early ray of April,

cats in the buxus tangling
with the butter-shadow.

A dream bundled with wheat
and un-cut grass — baking.

Lyric taking out my creases,
as I idly sweeten worry with a cigarette —

I could linger here in old indolence
like a green prophet.

Lazing the rest of my life
amongst this garden
whilst the world
pays its taxes.

No Happiness Left To Feed It

Despair is wide —
is always under-fed

I can fit all the happiness you
give me into it,

all the love ingests:

affection's glisten
gives the starving all it is,

the great pounding mouth,
looks jealous on

It can fit all all the grinning,
and in a split: void it

It is a fault
It is a fault I feed daily

I Cannot Keep You

My life is a small room
overlooking time

I often let flowers die,
I often lose friendships

You say I am young eyed
and boy'd of sorrow

(but my father left
— I cannot grow)

You stay a night —

our bodies make
the heat of sad planets

I write with the fog
of your mouth

I take the bus,
I miss stops,
I curl into the cinema
of your perfume

You say I am like
Peter Pan
(but my father left
— I cannot grow)

I often lose friendships
(I don't know why)

I often let flowers die,
(I sometimes know)

And you —
you have to go

My life is a small room
overlooking time —
I cannot keep you.

Love Develops in a Dark Room

Yearning glooms,

guiding an untaken photograph
to the protein of my cell —

splitting into image.

A face. A heart. A time.

This lonely room becomes
a theatre,

This lonely bone becomes
a stage for

all unsaid and played.

And I wonder if you
think of me.

And I wonder if you
lay alone,

even when he's
next to you.

Let Me in Beautiful Thing

You look for gaps — minor faults
and catastrophes in the golden
quarries of others —

somewhere your psyche might
fit — somewhere clean to hide
your filth — to stuff your minute
horrors in a washed paradise —
even if it breaks your bones —
even if you lose your health —

you try personalities — different
sounds — you practice the little
sermons you find in magazines
against the mirror — you try and
make your body fit — you hold
your body like a broken child —

you wonder if everyone feels
alone — if loneliness is bacterial
— infectious — if when you
speak they hear the shameful
caverns of your prayer — the
affirmations you find in the lyrics
of your favourite films —

you hate the promise sex offers
— you might die having to slam
your body like a moon into the
earth of others —

you have a prickling hope —
marketing mostly — that a new
jacket or fashion — new hair
— might burrow you in — fast
track to a speed like Doherty or
Cohen or Wainwright —

that there's something —
someone out there — like
Dickinson or Plath — that
someone has complete poetic
knowledge — that they see you
— say come in — you're hurt —
you're beautiful

V

The Boy Who Never Fell

A Boy Dies in the Rain

An arrangement of weather;
systems of light and water,
night and gale, cirrus —
nimbus claps its sorrow,
weeps and paints the starry view.
A view above a hospital.

I howl.

I cannot light my cigarette.
I hold my mothers hand.
A boy dies in the rain.

Daffadowndilly

The daffodils are dying;
lanterns dimly gasp,
blonde brass flicker whitely,
their sightly joy is faded,
stems are jaded in the grass —
they were shining once.

Seemed so brief.

Say —

what do I tell? When asked
how many brothers I have?

Do I say three? And lie?
Then recount the truth
and time you died?

Do I say two? And never say,
that we were three
but yesterday?

Seems too brief.

Tell.

What do I say Tom?
Now the daffodils are gone?
Shall I say I see them still?
Shall I say you're twenty one?

I can't.

That's too young — too brief

I Write From a Pale House

When I write about you —

it is less like a symphony — or light,
nor like glittering or the flush of gas.

Nor the symmetry of idol.

It is unlike the gloss,
or the great alarm of brain
spinning colour.

It is never the nursery,
never heaven's speak
released —

it is unlike sleep.

It is a glare — a hear of
hiss and boom. It is a
woeful lonely thing
full of sound and
remembering.

Your breath.

Your cold hand.

Every Lyric Is Harmed

Grief salts life,
nothing lives on it.

I used to write romances,
now I write futures —

I design with
fingers in the sand,
drive pictures into time

I wait for miracles
and neat paradises

I wait for Godot,
I wait for a light

(I wait to like my life)

I wait for fame —
for a starred night,
or the lemon of
an early wish

I wait for last faces;
lost words to
scrum the sea —

I wait for you

I want to know what
time does out there —
are you aged?
Are you safe?
Are you still
younger than me?

Items of a Familiar Haunting

There are years so long
they overlap —

I've had three Octobers
I've had Octobers in June
Octobers in traffic —
Octobers on a Christmas morning

(there is a candle still
lit from your birthday)

(we re-painted your room,
a decade — or last Thursday ago)

(tomorrow is a hanged hope)

You stare at doors when
you miss someone,
you wait at windows

What is a ghost?

It is not what they say

A ghost is a living,
musical thing —
it's a collision of wind
and photograph,
it is the similar shape
of stranger's head in the street,
it is two sugars in a cup
of tea — or The Libertines
on repeat —

A poltergeist is a puppet of grief —
It is a muscle pulling a
human bone through the
motion of a day

(I broke that glass,
I moved your
paining off the wall
I screamed these
names into this house)

A spirit;

it is a future that
lives in the family
and fixes them
to the past —

A haunting;

It is dreaming
for seven
years I could
have saved you —

release is sleeping
knowing I couldn't

That you would forgive me

That there was nothing to forgive

That you would want me
to have found this happiness --

that you are part of it

Scrying on a Christmas Bauble

Lights peck;
spotter green and white
the eye harvests dews
of golden bell —
the lance of winter spice

The damp-bright day
is alive to the surface

And you are there —

solid as a ghost
on gradient memory

It is just fantasy I know,
but I pull you from colour
and for one last time
this home is a home

this family a family

this Christmas — a Christmas.

Swallows

I was told swallows
follow the light to Heaven

and carry letters
in their murmur.

Well I am full of language —

but I cannot speak like that,
through death to truth

(it is hard to know you
and not know where you are)

I am too much these words
that were yours.

That I didn't get to say.

Like ***sorry.***

Like ***come home.***

There in the Blue

There in the blue,
(in the brilliant blue)
behind the ghost,
your hand like
the palest willow;
like a film of birch
stripped fine,
like a myth,
first Greek,
then refined,
then retold.
There in the blue
(in the brilliant blue)
behind the ghost
your hand
like the last of life,
reaches mine.

The Lantern

If from your gold
door you see
me crying,

do not tell me
not to weep,
or wipe these
eyes for me.

These are lucky tears
I have them won through
loving you —

and do not
mend my smile
it is not to be
repaired —

this is the
quiet of loss,
that comes from
being loved by you.

And if,
when standing
by your starry glass
you see me
leave a lantern on,

do not turn it off.
it is my light for you.

And do not say
you cannot come.

It is my light for you.

The Road Trip We Never Took

Ten years after your death —

I sit at my desk — there's a keel to my spirit — lowness — like muscle being pulled into earth — my words itch — I'm silent — I brood and avoid conversation — the sounds of a city scratching the planet — the dust of ignition in the nostril — the windows are greased with the oiled fractures of names — your name —

I'm thin and cellular — not really there — mist-blood, office politic — there's a phantom-solidness to thought — nothing — whooping sadness —

I leave early — I rarely cry — I sit in my car — my eyes stream —

I've not said your name out loud for years — I miss the conversations we had — the things that were swallowed into your death — that never came back out — things I waited for — that I hoped might reappear — the joy of video games — horror films — fast food reviews — sharing a book — they were mine as much as yours — ours — you never met my son — ***that hurts*** —

That's lonely — that's loneliness — that's isolation — it's half of myself forced into a quantum box — stuffed between the grains of your ashes —

It's too much — I'm breaking with space — calcifying with all the things I should have shared —

I look to the empty passenger seat — I think — I can pretend — believe you're here — that we're on a road trip — some adventure — finishing some unfinished-promise —

so I do —

I say — ***hey, Tom — how are you?*** I clip the seatbelt around your absent body —

I start the car —

I imagine we're on route 66 — or the winding trails of Ennerdale — or back near Mum's old house on a family trip to Somerset —

I talk — like you're there — I tell you about my son, about being a dad, how you'd have been a great uncle — that you'd have loved him — him you — I tell you about the shit films I've watched — the one's we loved to hate — that I heard there's a new Resident Evil game — I haven't bought it as there's no one to play with — that I might tonight — we could play it together — I tell you we've still not spoke to Dad — that he didn't come to your funeral — never came back to England at all — I tell you that I'm sorry that I never finished your script — that it was too hard to read your work — that at some point I'll be brave enough to publish your writing —

I drive for an hour — the motorway speeds — seventy — eighty miles an hour —

I cry the entire way — it's half-happiness, it's years of love, of still wanting to be your big brother —

It feels precious and foolish — like all magic feels to adults — like all wonder does at first —

I calm myself as I near the end of the road — ten seconds from home — drop to first gear —

I slow the car almost to a stop — I say — it's time — I've got to go home — you have to go home — I reach to your seat and unclip your seatbelt —

then the car — mere feet from the house — abruptly stops — as though I've hit something — the shock wakes me — drags me back — I try the engine — but it won't move — it lurches as though stuck —

I climb out the car — look to see if I've missed something in the road — a large stone — or obstruction —

the entire front axel has come off — the front wheels are no longer connected to the car —

I call an emergency mechanic — I've only had the car a week — he looks at me —

You've just come off the motorway? He asks — he whistles — folds his brow —

Yeah — I reply

He holds up the bolt that should be connecting the axle —

This wasn't on properly — he says — *you've been sold a death trap — if this would've come off on the motorway, you and probably whoever was behind you — you'd have been dead* — he clicks his fingers — *never seen anything like this* —

It's a miracle you're alive mate — he scratches the sweat from his head — *you must have someone watching over you* — he looks to the sky — I look to the empty passenger seat —

you okay? He asks —

you look a little shaken up

VI

The Comet Sweeper

Your Beauty Reaches the Sky

There must be design;

in you is a geometric happiness,
in you is the fuel that tends the eye;

that famed symmetry —
that sweet goad that
drags men to graves of war

or taunts them to build a
chapel and spoil their time,

or in some mid-summer arcade —
gladly crack their necks and gaze
into the mythed-birthplace of the sky
and title things they cannot touch —

to graze their lives with yours
till they are red enough to die

You Say Write Simply

Sorry.

You say write simply.

But even your shadow is a beauty,
I watch it clamber walls
and flush their shape.

I eye its drape on
furniture when you talk.
It shimmers at the edges
when you laugh,
I sometimes take its memory with me
to the bath when I drink alone.

It can mute a prism's show.

I know. You say write simply —

but I am floored
by how light it feels to
know you.
I don't float — I vaporise.
mingling with Argon
in your breath,
and I don't fear dying, but death —
the ending vision of my hour.
(If you're the view at its beginning.)

Sorry.

But my words ease through stained
glass as I look through you to speak.
they are confused as they pass —
they think are fiction.
Even my diction thinks it's a bird.

Sorry. You say write simply.

So — I like how life looks now you're here.

The Comet Sweeper

Then how lovely
is your normal beauty?

In your eye is the
slade that heaven seeks —
— a place to put its
peace — or release
its poetic science

Your body is the ordinary
lesson hormones teach,

the stelliform
beyond a blink's reach —
the dark mink of mind's
normal animal —

everything you think normal
reminds me I'm a witness —

here to ticket
freckles on your skin —
here to sweep comets
off your sweetness.

The Bride of Life

What if I were honest,
and said you are not
what you seem?

That I hear names,

that you have colours
light hasn't yet
dreamed.

That naked you are
a strobe
to sad sleep

that you are the
atom the
apple meets?

That love is mind
and bone,
it is earth and vision
driving fire through
a whooping night.

So then,
would it be okay?
would it be alright?

If I said,
that I see you twice;

as body and
as the bride of life.

I Am No Architect

I cannot paint like light can;
cannot speak like spectrum's bow,
nor scatter prisms on our skin
with fingers, tongues, or sight.

I cannot make a vision
from a tapestry of light.

Though try I might —

I cannot blend the dell
in a sweep of spectral heaven,
nor pick the airy fruit
in an angel's bay of lemon,
or a garden of God's iris -

and I write of spiders, death and insects,
as much as ruin, love, or violence —

I scale —

I climb words trying to build your
beauty — to make a view of what it is to
be seen — to be known —
to be loved by you

I Am a Lovely Insect Tonight

She has caught the earth,
and given it to my eye,

look how my body
rises with the rain —

I am thyme,
garlic, mint.

It does not matter
if I am the boozy
slink of earth
under her boot.

I say crush me,
I say wet me,

I love the world.

A Memory Forms in Its Crib

It is a firmament you make;

in a Smith's tee,
knots of hair, the rush
of celled blush to your cheeks

your arched back like
birch — silvered
with wet natures

there are dimples in the
glee you share —

The Cure, Joy Division,
the hidden meanings
in Pink Floyd's albums

you unravel them as
a child does a birthday,
or the scientist does
a shell —

holding your intellect
to me — prying
the spiced darks of life

— if I am quiet enough,

beneath silence there
is the rhythm of memory
crested — the tattooing
of a mark to the Earth's time

a picture I can come back
to when I forget how
lovely it is to live

A River Writes Our Poetry

The Mersey bakes — it murmurs
in the heating of its body,
a willow skins its species of leaf
and makes drowned
puppets on the water,

their lime agonies
wrapped in stick and
the gangrenes of human plastics,

the sun gores through,
pulling watered
poetry into the hazes
of summer —

the scent excites the mosses
and the midges have their
orgies on the limbs we tie
trying to make one body
from two bodied skins

Your Body Is My College

I could find any inch of you
in paradise —

I have learnt you — through
endless sleeps and human knots,

through playing — as play
is, to two fox cubs in the wood,

through study — as study
is to the botanist — who
knows poisons and the
health in natural worship —

if you were lost — lost yourself
in some maddening — or deep
cut of low love,

I could find your atom's
atom in any crevice of
my blood and give back to
you the beauty of your life

Trying To Write a Love Poem

You are made of such common things,

of the same bored mineral as I am,

and even those un-dreaming things —
the copse, the steeping fell,
the glassy inlands thieving rain,

yet you are so unalike.

So un-seeming of the same.

There is a race for my word
to compare you to blossom,
or fire, or tanzanite.

But too much falter for me to write it.

It would be too little.

This Normal Garden

I might embarrass Buckthorn,
make pink pea — blush tulip,
or green rose as it gloats
begging to be beheaded.

If I were to lay —

Split myself, and score my blood
amongst the garden.
let the birds peck
my frame away.

All unsaid would lush —
remnants left would say —

a note about your mind,
or an outline of your wit,
your voice (its ghostliness
when dreaming). The hour
of your efforts and ambition,
your humour and delighting.
The elegance of charity,
as you imagine kindness.

If I were to lay, and out these words,
no one would notice this garden.

Love Inside a Paper Heart

If I could;

envelope the sky, salt air
with line I've writ,

soothe ire with lip and
gift the contents to your heart

If I could;

flirt the light — bring
the shadow glooming home,

stay the agony of the daffodil
in its spectral crest alight

Then might you see —

I love and loved you more

That I would have wreaked
all nature

to show you are lighter — lovelier.

Time's Lovely Attic

Give me your hand —

with your fingers
I could count
apples, or skies

I could clean
the lonely
night men are
born through

Look on me —

between your eyes
I could proof
the lie I've
told of life —

(that there is
magnificence)

an hour near your
mouth and I'd spin
your breath through
a myth

so that in lives
away they'll sing
your name through
tubes on Mars —

I don't need
you to love me —
I've been loved,

I've made
pillows for it,
it dreams
elsewhere

just let me stay
between you,
let me write
you something,

I could take you
from time's attic
and stand you on
a word —

not fragile
like — promise

but a good solid
verb —

like, dying

and show you from this
book and say —

look —

I have told truths —
a life exists in her
worth living for

A Dream Whilst Breathing Light

Man nurses the visions
you give —

that's what he keeps
when at distress
and all the good
seems drawn away —

it is his key to the prison
of a mundane day —

it is the memory of
flesh that makes
him dream

he can love a thousand
times from a chance

live forever on the edges
of love if he must

Man's peace is in his head,

like rain is hazel's
swollen secret

love is pressed upon
the inward eye till
it is wet with happiness

And it is this;

your intellect,
your summer dress,
your ageing lines,
your artfulness,

that man takes with him
over to to his shiny death

and then through
onto to the next —

when he is stone or a
grain within the brook
or the soaring lush of kite —

or just a flower
in a field who waits,

who dreams of
you whilst
breathing light

This House We Make in the Wood

It would not be a waste
to waste here;

we would make a darkly orphaned
house on this soil where our bodies
love upon —

and leave bubbled rooms for the rain,
and shade where shadow shone

and from this graze — the dark
and dazed — children of the wood would come —

light would gasp in the fingered lane
where our nails have gladly gone —

and the score of hip, would
trip the hare when that
happy death has won —

this trench we make,
would call the spiders with
our bodied drum —

and the fox and doe,
would know this space
as a place to kill and run —
by the windows of this house
we've made of the love we once begun,

and from that waste —which is not a waste
— but the song of loving done --

the last English Elm might grow
and soar it's pleasures to the sun

Lessons From the Atom of Your Eye

Should they ask —
I will blame my
happiness on you,

even my solemn
thoughts are plum

my fingers dance
when I text
I am nervous
all the time —

look — I have
luck again,

I have chance I might
learn something
through you —

something worthy
of a poem —

like this;

blonde has a thousand
suns — it belongs to lovely
things —

your name is a purse,
it flirts my life into it

A Kitchen Mid-Atlantic

You stir the pot — exist
simply —

I don't look on you,
I gaze —

I am seized by the
spheric magic of
time's time —

I see;

all my coloured pencils,
my late night strays,
my teenaged sorrow —

you are the happiness
I hurried in the wood,
the letter I wrote and
stuffed into the blank
palace of a tree when
I was seven —

you are the lost host
of my childhood heaven

with you I am a small
body in the reed,
skin gored and pleased
by midge and nettle —

with you there is the
feel of sunlight to a
thousand grazed knees —

the disease of magic
that lingers in the
artist's head

to be with you
ruins reason

it makes me
want to love you

it makes me think
old things,

to say we were once
awake in an early night,
as two items in a cell —

that we were playmates
in that first agony
of imagination —

the last shone as
it broke and dreamt
of doing human things

VII

I've Held You in My Arms As the Thing That Time Wants

A View From Below Your Heart

To the great feminine,

the curling pattern,
the drifting shadow
swarming on the
kitchen floor —

guiding all the spiders
to the brimming of
a sleeping tint —

tainted hope.

Below.

Stay the glooming,
female spirit,

life looks down
on me as a crypt.

I look up on love
as a door.

I want out.

The Futurist's Museum

Then my love might become
an article — a peculiarity
for some futurist's museum.

Splayed against an organ,
or the pickle of some bone.

Or an artefact, by the brain,
by some rotted grecian throne.

Then my love might become
an attraction — a ward
to stray a gleeing.

A bane against some
distant eye,
dyed towards a dreaming.

Who thinks —

whilst leaning in to touch —

I too knew love.

Once.

My Body Calls to Space Inside You

Tulip swells pulling sun;
prickled with colour,
his hallow stem thirsting
— ***my fingers do***

Plates shift, strain, jolt —
yet leave salt remaining
in the fixture of the earth.
It keeps shape
— ***my heart seldom does***

Your body flirts with light
            changing decoration,
pasteling like church pane
            fraught with summer

And I must remind myself
that this is just a window,
casting light upon your body

The Heart Is the Body's Anemone

The heart grows in the red-
garden of the body, it sows its
dreaming root and takes the
human as its full host — the
lover as its atmosphere. Its
synthesis is through sense;
the miraculous sound, the
astonished eye, the temperate
touch — all feed its little hopes.
It stows memory, it sets its
histories into the head; then
the legs and fingers, then the
arms and organs, till even the
bone is flowered-flush with silly
detail; dates, colours, names —
futures.

A heart cannot break — it
is not brittle — it is a living
heaving thing. When love falls,
it is the human-light that goes
out. And in that long-dark,
it gasps on the remnants of a
ghost. It lives like an anemone
in a ruined house — still
breathing with its seed asleep
— till a song, or scent or
photograph breaks through and
it leans again and reaches for
the residues of the life it had
hoped.

Nature Carves Itself in Your Image

There are birds
on your lingerie —
they are brightly lifted

Noon gulps shadows
from your surface —

I fasten my breath
to your lips

Are you beautiful?

No

No, you are the river
the ice mourns.
You are the lonely
thing the fox looks for.
You are the woman
the stone wants to be.

Icarus Flies Too Close to Your Love

There's a day
on your skin,

you are mineral-peach,
you are happiness
to a tongue —

between your hip,
I write wet philosophy,
pulling human songs
from your chest

(it is the beauty of
death that rolls
from you)

the throat swells
like a coral moon

I fill my hands
with the pink
waters of your skin

I am a man
dreaming of motion

Icarus fell
I might too

You Make Eden's Where You Lay

It's evening;
landscape-skin-pastel,
we're sticky-hot with god —
nothing is nude enough,
there's always too much cell.

We share tea and cigarette,

the city ricks itself with shadow
the stray cats sing something darkly;

Wonder Wall — Sing Hossana —

it never matters
sound clots our lungs;
your lip is apple-cannabis,
our teeth clink like moths in spring,
Johnny Marr is creased,
tangled with knicker
in the corner of the room.

I think you are the
damp of prophets
lovely as a hymn

You say it's just a myth,

you say Woman makes herself.

Noon-light trims your hip
paints you cotton,
I ticket fingerprints across you —
you are smaller than the earth.

I know you are right.

Cats Sing Darkly of Me

Yet light didn't die —
(not today)

cats
sing darkly of me,

through slits, they garner
all my suffer

and spread it to the
garden,

telling lilly and the
iris

to abandon when I
pass —

all,
think darkly of me —

all,
whisper when I drift —

yet light didn't die
(not today)

— you just left
(and haven't said when you'll
be back)

Between Your Lovely Valley

Tonight the tongue is my
entire body

Your body the entire
Earth

My lips
move like tropics
across your gleaming thigh
and to the atom of your
human tincture

I'd be happy here
to the ends of time,
in the rosed bower of
of your legs.

My humid brain in your
humid cradle — fluttering
as I push my
poems through you.

In a Summer Garden

Crescent shadow cradles lash,
lid dusks — iris slips and caps,
— crowning jade.

Right sight rays, stays in light,
incubates a starry heath,
— Saturn's maid.

Your hand cups —

bough of fingers shade,
and bring your lips to breath.

Summer ghosts across the lip.

Yes that is death —

in this memory you never turn,
you lie between seething grass,

Always still.
Always tired.
Always some excuse.

That's what love becomes.

A poem.

Last Night I Dreamt

Yesterday I was darkly set,
and milled about the house

and in my fingers found
it hard to write,

and had stayed past the
hour where sorrow eats the night.

And in that inching dream,
I remembered Manderley,

and your red dress,
and your shoes in
the rain

and in feeling glad,
felt sad again

Let's Starve Together

Do no wait with me inside,

come;

strip and teach your throat
toward my hand,
let me lean it skyward.
Unbolt your teeth,
wide jaw, bare breasted,
come gain this wet and awful spectre.

Clutch at each of my
posing bones, and lead
your agony into mine.

Let me make of you
a great suffering thing.

Then;

lay with me,
feel how starving it is —
to be perishing always.

How hot it is.

Travels Along Your Inner Zodiac

My skin waits for your salt,
it cuts with your perfume

your word is capsicum
to the throat

my tongue cramps,

I want your name in my mouth —

it is love that scares this poem,
my fingers moth, they march to
your light

It is the kiss of nettle,
the brace of bramble
you leave behind

Yet they are kinder,
they leave a rash —
you have cleaned my gasp,

my joy starves,
my art is a bird
against the glass —

Let me in,

I am stale without you

I want you back

I want to feel that planet in you

I am too close to the soil
when we touch

Perfume Therapy

Your perfume can be a paper-cut
— an ident to the side of line.
It can be a recharging or a gunshot,
a wound in time re-breaching

The beseeching of a memory
to gain its blood back in

It can make — it can ruin my day

Depending on the chemical

I Like it When We're Invisible

It is early and we are dying,

I say do not sleep —

so we stay as vanishers do
and watch the night
decay and break —

everything is light scare;

every slanted roof,
and cigarrette,
every branded jean
and smart phone,
every I owe you
and promise
belongs to going

Tomorrow is a hinge
and needs a push —

and we don't hold hands
because we're closer apart,
nearer when not in ruin —

and we weep as lyric does
(dry-wide like beach
spreading for the moon)
because no one else sees her
— mother

the one a child knows
before face —
the one he finds alone
on a rooftop,
or in the scum
of his fingernail
searching soil for tooth —

that one

The Potato

We're busily lost — finding new
landscapes to cross tongue
— tap finger — lick — taste,

the house is a mess —
song slips between
a pale smoke — room
to room and under
the inch-shade beneath
a door — along a gasp —

we live on each other;

like oxygen
and carbon-dioxide
gummed with sweat
and bodily soil —

there's a potato we
left in the cupboard,

it's grown flaxen —
has long ghostly
arms — it sulks in
a turquoise clot

there's no time
to clean it up —

there's too much
of you to know

The Thing That Time Wants

I've held you in my arms
as the thing that time wants,

there are no guesses to
its work —

look at starlets, or Camelot,
look at the spoiled fruit
on the mantle, or that
neighbour to whom
no one knocks —

I write, so I can steer —
so I might flirt my
chance ahead

Years —
I've seen it purl your hair,

decades —
you'll forget me

or I'll lose my head —

having gone too far through
with this art —

and I will come to
this wood,
by this rank tree
and find our mangled name

And I'll write
this poem
for the soil —

the worm will
lift the nitrates
and pull

swollen flowers
from the ground,

strike bramble
from the earth
and wreck the
forest with
your colour

It will be a place
poets lie and
write histories —

they'll find your fame
between their fingers

Time will not have you

VIII

Tomorrow - Forever

The Poltergeist

You are just a poltergeist

It is your philosophy,
that in the endless
years when you are gone,
will take your child's
and lead them
through a darkened night.

It is todays love
that drives
their tomorrow on —

it is your art now that
will spire the dawn
of a new mind whose
time has come,

or in the distant litters of
your voice —
your words are the
bloodless friend a
book becomes,

or the mending to
a broken heart
who finds hope
where there was none.

***You too
are possessed.***

Your smile is the
apparition
of your mum,
you dance to
an ancestral
drum,

or by the gravity of
work left by eras
come and gone.

No —
life's spectre
is never done.

Some have wounds
from wars
centuries on.

Or cold spots
of grief
that families write
their lore upon.

The present
lives along
the spool
of history,

it is here
the spectral
future's spun.

What you give
is gifted or taken
from the sum.

You may think you
have no meaning,
you may think
you do not matter,

but it is your today
that is the
ghostly clatter,
it is your sob and weep
your joyful laughter

that is the sound
of tomorrow
and every hereafter
after this.

And though the earth
is just a sleeping
arrow shipping
dreamers to the sun —

what you move
moves still —

what you live —

what you
did, didn't,

couldn't,
could've —

what you
think you lost
what you love —

it all
lives —

it all haunts on

Let's Hide in This Moment

Do not share this moment -
no, to share would be to shred,
would be to take the pulp,
the sacred from its scalp.

No one needs to know,
nor hear about this here,

it could live — you see —

it could linger only now
and vanish between
our two heads —

Wouldn't that be rare?
Wouldn't that be something?

That this moment here was
known by us — lived by us
alone.

How beautifully insignificant
we would become?
How dangerous, and wild.

To be unfamous things —

To be private heroes
in an un-read life

Something I Have Not Touched

It is the domestic
treasure of my head
to drive pleasure mad

to think and think
and think —

till pleasure
itself is sad.

To make
the comic of
existence graphic —

to think
and then think —

to take pain
into bed,
and fuck peace
in its wet song,

to suckle weed from
the lovers I've had
as though their
waste could clean
some wasted sympathy.

It is love, I make
my quilted
worry from.

It is worry I build
my calendar on —

it is panic I put upon
the tumbling cells
of a sleep.

It is my nature
to harm the
healing had,

to think under
the scab
their might
be some petaled
line — or a clean
image of holy love

— a red memory
in my perfumed skull
that waits intact,

something I
have not
touched.

Antique Memories of Our Time

The fading memory has its beauty too,
its image has the sharp coo of frost

the things I forget are green things
ticked by an old shine —
they have the beauty of a ghost

and on them faces of frozen youth,
or the aged-imagining which is still
more beautiful than truth —

but it is a truth still — more lovely still —

if it is not, then I would go
about my day unmoved

yet — look

I sail on hours like a goose

I stare and peck from stillness
lives and endless lives
and life — so much

A Library of Faults

I may never repossess peace,

I try and make a space for you
by turning the volume down
or watering the flowers
or drinking herbs —

there were so many warnings,

literature is a library of faults;

men dangling their broken
bones — flashing their
sorrows like naked temples.

Come in and learn they said.

I didn't.

Some Things Remain

Things remain from childhood;
scars, sadness, shadow — fright

Some trials etch & alter braveness,
some aisles of darkening will the light away
— even when you reach

Some things from childhood teach
you sorrow; the death of childhood
pets, friends gained and lost,
a parent's love once waning — gone
— a family now a ghost

Some things remain from childhood;
hope, heart, home — delight.
some trails etch and alter braveness,
some tales of brightening will
away the dark — even when you're weak

And even on the softest day they speak —
listen —

some things from childhood reach
and strain their hour
from the bower yesterday
and lighten out the crease

Some things remain from childhood —
some do not

Some things remain from childhood —
the others I've forgot

Gazan Birds

Gazan birds are red,
their feathers gone.

Night falls like spears
onto children's beds.

Mothers are soft
and not built for bombs.

They wrap their infants
with their skin.

Lullabies are delicate,
they never reach the ear
before sleep has come.

The airs are hot,
kerning time —

— sulfur bores through
childhood — it smoulders
generations on.

And on.

And on.

I smoke as much
as I want. My death
is in the future.

Puck on the Thistle

The night casts oddly
bronzed people
on the wall —

with residential humour
it aligns the forgotten
futures that played
yesterday's head —

I was a child ten lifetimes ago

It was a dark-aged hope
that I might have lived like
that racing newt —

or like the Puck upon
the thistle with her
gushy dress —

I was never young —

I was born with this old
harm in my head —

I cannot be
what I want to be —

I have forgotten
what that is

Human Pollen

It may be, that the night's silver
hive, will move as happy as a bee
to the pollen of our lives
and carry us to our mothers

— who never died

— but wake in folded night,
tucked between the honey-glen
of death which is not death
but another style of life

And that our bodies and these
bodily delights were parcels
for a magic sleep —
little costumes made for
play — and we see that
everything decays
in some sort of sweetening
— some cooking of a life

Where every atom plays the part
of every thing with shape

and our hundred names
and times were one
on a stage —

some part of a comedy,
or tragedy,
or history

Still Your Child

I am still your child,
and you are not gone;

I was risen in the lamp
of your room,
the heat from you
is the heat in me.

The heart I have
is half of yours
and I am still your child
for you are not gone

So the life of you
is never done
as I am made of you

And though you sleep,
you wake with me
and walk as I walk on

For I am still your child
(forever your child)
and you are never gone.

To a New Mother

All things seem twined.

The spirt of elm begins
childing in the soil,
gains mothering in the sky.

The sparrow parent twice flies,
the mother has duet of eyes
and gains a glee of second sight.

And no night is lone,

and no fearful symmetry
roams the iris
or glooms the view.

All now is new.

The earth gives a gift to mothers.

You will see with two hearts,
and love twice the things
you once forgot.

Pink Little Orchard

Longing gives long sight —

and from the hour of my work,
I can vision all your shape.
Draw the gold and skin
and appear you at my desk.

I can scene you,
never needing note,

I remember bright weed;

dandelion leaning,
neat blush — daisy
curling finger. Purslane
smarting to be between
your toe. Lambsquarter
glad to die beneath you.
My own dashing ideal,
tousled into graves of blonde.

The slipping dress
giving look to collar,
lips naming children
we might someday have

(Can we?)

(I love the name Olive.)

(I imagine you round,
and sweet and full)

For You Are Bright

Then you are bright and I am a bower,
where light reposes or stretches with
glassy arms towards your life

So then you are bright —

So then I am poor and dark,
and in constant conflict —

and seek host for word;
seek most of words
riches in the belly
of life's fruit

And care not for truth
but glory,
of story in this bask
of being,
marrow in the art
of seeing and
adding it to verse

So then I am a curse,
and you are the nurse
between the light —

For you are bright

And indent the sky —
which indents this page

For you are bright

Mimic of a Lonely House

Our house misses you;

it re-scents satin,
and sits your shadow
in a pastel
on your favourite seat

It says I remember;

and mimics your
footstep in the night.
pipes breathe,
tiles temper rain
like fingernails on
a screen —

it says I grieve,
and spiders
stitch up grief —
and moth
thinks you're
quartered up in light,

each nook expands,
and holds out its
space for you to home

— but you do not return,

so the house says —

I am a church now

and we hang
your picture
by the tulip

Lamplighters

When I am brokered,
and these histories
are played out on some last
fantastic radio —

some scene of science fiction,
where the narrator with
his tin-light tongue
says - *that's it* —

that's all,

Our hero has to go —

and I am unset from my
box and given back to you;

given blackly to that
living street where all
the hurtings slow,

I'll say —

It was hard to play alone

and the streetlights
loft-high-low,
will with their litter glow

and all the other children
will to their homesteads go,

and we shall stay —
for we have nowhere
else to go,

and no one else will say a thing
as there is no one else to know

for I am given back to you

Parsifal

Un-still is life; stars wilt,
stones lose their name to time,
flowers have their tincture leak,
oceans have their fame diminished,
sparrows lose their twinkled speech

Sun has her waning ebb
and will perish like a bud,
gods and angels strain
and spread like the
smoke of faithful love —

(gone)

the nightingale, builds her nest,
and sings a score or ten,
till the kitten in the garden grows,
and steals away her den

Comets trail towards the heart,
yet miss the blood and bone,
they sweetly skim the web of life
like a gazer's skipping stone —

hissing into gas

Un-still is life — nothing lasts

Men die — in triumph or in loss,
their love's labour never found —
Hamlet is slain — Ophelia drowns

Yet I am deathless — I am glossed
in this embrace —
as you are now upon this page

Your loveliness curling with
these words on a distant
strangers tongue flickering back to life —

my word is mass — yet

un-still is love — nothing lasts

The Greatest Poems

The greatest poems
are not in a book,

they live in birthday cards,
and mobile phones,
and post-its on the fridge —

See —

the true poem comes
to the brick-layer
who has never writ
- yet finds a
a simple verse
for his wife when
she's ill or feels
forgotten

It is the art from
the child who forms
an abstract image
of his mother
and she realises
she is colour
and bright

Or it is the mural of the
the starry night on a
nursery by a new father
who doubts his skill,
but hopes to be
a better man —

it is the off the cuff
bedtime story
that stirs the mind
in boyhood - and to
adulthood on and on

It is the photo of the
family still complete
or the frame of
someone missed,
willing with you
out the door

Poetry — art —

it is the I miss you mums,
the come homes, the
I saw this and thought
of you, or I am reminded
of your favourite colour
today — and felt sad,
but happy too

These are the greatest lines,
these are the life-won
arts of intimacy,

of knowing and
being known

And if you are lucky
enough to share
a home and have
the eye to see it —

yours is a gallery
and all the poetry
with it

Onward!

Onward decay, onward bright
and fearing, onward spoil and
ruin and leaving ray. Onward
toward the end of day, onward
on tomorrow till tomorrow
splits and in garish heat erupts
and evaporates. I say onward
nothing, and everything, and
all blood in my heart and all
my bone that has gained from
soil to grain again to sand
and go. I say onward pleading
eye, onward naivety. Onward
bravery and hero, onward meek
and any daring brain that seeks
to pair this loss, and stands
forward in the night and leans
themselves against the death
and says remember me.

You are not yet Born

If I could — I'd curl my hands
— make a cove of them to hold you —

and lead you through the footsteps
I softly left whilst sleeping —

lift you past the thorny sun,
to night's starry aspen house,
to its ashen windows streaming

and say — light —

you and this child are both alike,
both seed-asleep and dreaming

both waiting to be named

Please — keep this one safe

daphne

IX

Daphne

Fire in the Groves of Spring

There's the static-dream of wine round my cells — the pygmy-warming of particles in my brain — thoughts last longer — they ooze — honied and thick — it's my birthday tomorrow — I drift round Florence — move through its ancient body — it peaches in the sun — everything has a ginger pleasure to it — like it's made from the grains of a postcard — the joy inside a glass jar of marmalade —

it has been years since I've been moved — since I've allowed myself to be astonished —

I head into the Uffizi gallery — inattentive — committed to being part of the swarm — following the bobbles of hair and head — headphones mewing

— past time — through time — art — statue — the ghostly residue of eyes — the limerick visions of dead-heads on every wall —

I see it all — though don't really see — it sort of glances — numbed — pretty grazes that don't ident memory —

I step into a shallow room — behind the grasses of a crowd — the gurgled murmurs of polite boredom — and I see it — the painting — it strikes my hormone from a brute sleep —

Boticelli's Primavera —

I gasp — take in life through my teeth — I quiver — rattle in the firmament of shock —

there's something — something singing — something living in its groves — its laurels — its goddesses — a high terrible beauty in its yanking spirit that spits a fire to my eye — re-twists a sorrow — a wide-meaning I had not remembered I had lost —

I stand for a minute — for ten — for twenty — a solid sufferer in a watery crowd — I'm there a thousand lifetimes at its spectral house —

I want to weep — to say thanks — to kneel — to scrape the

worship from my organs and give it to this view — have it all — everything —

I've been sleeping — I am alive — I am alive — I am alive — I am alive —

I am awake

Daphne

Quiet -

Say ever loud world louder

Say speak —

Say I am silent anatomy loud.
Say I am the calcium phosphorus
of your church.

Say I am Cadmium, Chloride, Antimony.
Say I am your stainable vision.

Say divine horror mark me.

Say I am man's extinguished eye re-lit.
I am the childhood brain alive.

Say I am the romantic imagination.

Say tired wonder — un-tire.
Say I am victory,
I am mouth.
I am the fingers
that will write you

Say Daphne —

Can you hear me?

Say yes —

Say I am modern man
here to resurrect you

Grounding in a Stolen Wood

Make an altar
on a pitch of grass,

take off your shoes and let
the human foot find
its human root

and down the sun comes
spicing antique thoughts
on your breath —
till its action is peace

now trembling hymns
are coming to fill the
crevice of a day

Stay

Bask until your
brain is tin-coloured
and has in it
a little room for
love and more love
— and more love still

and endless fields
of fantasy

Look,

you are not fixed —

nothing is moored,

the stone of the riverbed
will make its way to
the sea

The Last Human Years

They say these are the last human years,
so lay your brain to waste with mine —

skittle your bone
slew your body
brake your tongue

let us lake this last,
this brief wonder
of ours and rake it.

Let us dream pink —

before reason shakes the final angel
from her hive,
and all the nooks of England
have rid of their drakes
and the faerie bowers have
had their light spent.

Let's spend it —

let us waste our years
in this lovely rot
and lend the finch
our lip - make
poetical all the
sounds of planet —

let us be kind to spiders
in this house, and know
the great strays gently.

Let us say — leave us be —
let us die as human things
before we can be uploaded
or upgraded and replaced.

Let us say,

let us stay naive,
childlike and breakable
unfixed and dumb
blind and bright
and full of hurt —

let us
suffer this last
human dream before
the night is out

Oozings From a Magic Cataract

The child knows;

if she squints, she can shake
the secrets from the earth —

teeming is a night — angels fall
in silky vehicles, comets scrape
the sherbert paradise off of its
candied hood —

in vestibules of half-sleep,
the magic of the day is cooked,
she squeezes from the solid
hour the soaring wounds of life —
magic oozes and oozes —

she can trace the sticky
spectre of a hope to its host —
she has no wish for clean — for dumb sight —

the adult to her seems already
dead — too joy proofed —
too cremated is his head —

she will say things like she
doesn't want to grow up —

what she means is she doesn't want to
give in — to let go of a roaring,
restless beauty —

she doesn't have to —

nor do I — nor do you

Beware the Disenchanted Traveller

Man — rid of his habitat,
will show you his ordinary day;
his brick and vehicle,
his letters on the wall —
his polite dream-proof children,

he will waste upon his fortune,
his ideas of victory and never
leave his office or enter his mind —

he will never dare to win the
effects of pansy to his psyche,

or the glades upon his pains —

or know the apparitions of
his imaginings as he knows
the celebrities of men

And he'll never spend a human day —

never see a ghost,
or the shadows of his loss,
or lose himself to beauty —
or his brains to high romance

He will show you this,

he will swear witness to
all monotony and materials,
never having heard the horn
or seen the stones at Gower —

and say there is no meaning,

do not believe him —

there is

The Human Insect

Head into the
dark stomach
of the wood
and lay in
its insect pits;

rinse in
a deep tide
of shade
till you are cleaned
of body;
till your fingers
are varnished
like bark,
— legs
like looms of
sickled air —

till you are just a
brain — a philosophy
in a basin of endless
deaths —

that thing before
your mother loved
you in her cells.

What do you see?

You are not alone.

Woman, Bite the Atom

Woman, bite the atom —

man has plucked
his philosophies
from their soils —

he germs them in
a lab — scales his music
scores his sex — gores
the melody of himself
and maims his eye
with holographic fictions…

He cannot see you —

Woman —

show your science
your earth, your filth,
show him those dank
nests fit for a poet's
brain —

stay him from that
clean glistening death —

remind him,

the chemical of
all things was brooded
in a waste —

whittle the stoic from him,
burn him —
and make his life
an instrument —

a thing for gods again

Make of him a great sufferer

A Complete Atlas for a Wounded Actor

After life —

we might come to that
child-like-locus — that
singular point of holy
dreaming —

and seed-asleep,
in our scorched crib —
with our mineral-less
body —

see everything as it is —

a spheric atlas,
— immense echo,
in a swarming oil
of light —

that there was never
a love lost — nor
child gone too soon
— nor a fracture to
life's beauty —

that it is all
complete —
all begun and
ended

starting at
its final point

Death in the Emeral Fire

To the wood —

it is the green headed
childhood horn

lovers have their first gasps
between the stick
their skin plucked
by the dirty glint of bramble

their heads wild —

grown wilder and
wilder still by love

the filthy bowers
have ingrown-dark

men dive their brains through
the nettle and the mint

Their pores boiling with violent
garlic and the sweat of vagrant grasses
and the dream of women in their beds —

They come to write skin,

They see the wetness of the pond or in
the mouth of herring
and know they cannot drink

It teaches them.

Puddle With a View of Heaven

The rain is
eating streetlight as it falls,
exhuming something from the ground

— not pretty enough to make a picture.

I should be outside
in a puddle
digging romance with it,

naming a new goddess,
or designing a ritual
to alter fault,
or breach bleeding
in my heart.

I should be outside,

wilding — barking,
instead of wondering
what else awakes —

I should be outside,

returning youth
to its master,
returning wonder
to its nature

The Famous Bones of Hero

There you are —
come to steal
the peace of men.

Your beauty dives their thinking
they are sweetened too much

their matter froths,
breaking like grog in the sea.

They have salt in their lives

I've seen their eyes saturnine

they love you cruelly and
sail their bodies down

the waves hurry to their
famous bones

They are
never complete again —

and I am just like them

(Lately my brain is staffed
with miracle — am I sick?
Am I sometimes
strange to touch?)

Wait with me

I have not come to know you
I have come to waste my talents

Begin - a Play

Begin.

A girl.

Makes a fissure in the night;
divine feminine keen
like a glooming blade,
wails and cuts the
cloud in two

— out glares a god,
un-woken till
that split.

A boy.

Draws with fingers,
the arcade of his
vision then
dies in the rain,
and leaves a book

— out glares a god,
un-moved by
his passing

— retires.

End scene.

Re-open.

Same girl.

Strews pigweed
off a bridge,
stuffs light between
her chest,
and drinks.

Same boy.

Drifts above his skin
along a braided stream.
His flesh splitting
into pattern.

Different God.

Slips off his
crystal brim,
and falls into
the decaying mouth.

The boy wakes.

On Looking Out to Sea at Night

Night's berry, white and brave
prickles in the upward bay,

fields bloom bright against the day,
its looming beam now bows.

Its fingers pluck and snug and twang
and sing with petrels over land,
as petals; silver, gloom and blush.
As nebulae fluoresce and bush.

Hush —the dark it croons,

Life hangs above the sea

And makes the thought of sleep — ill.
And makes the sleeping thought — awake.
And wakes the dreaming man — alive.

Oh, Sweet Mortal

I say love — it has made me better.

Not love towards a body
not that decay —
not the love of flesh
or the culling of sane
movement —
not a brief obsession with
hot skin.

No, I say — I love —
and it has made me better.

The earth, her, it, him;
eating soil in the night.
Stony teeth of worm
and bird —
the savage ray
cutting Yorkshire
like a neck —
the flower saying I am better
than weed then
nettle stewing its bone
(then bee straws its last light
and a child spreads
it on his toast)

That love, yes.

Oh, I want to live.
I really do this time.

Primavera

Botticelli,
I miss your starry forest —

my heart is with your women.

See — I am a maker too,
and dye the world like this;

thick melting nights,
hundred skinned plants
high romancing skies

I name everything —

man wants me to think
I'm metal -

but then my boys remind me I am
a plant,

and your paint shows me I am
not just jaw and waist.

I am a gardener
I am spit and puddle
and grow angels
and woody spirits
and make love last
and bloom pillars
from my salt —

see, now the night is baste,
the day loves and kills
and nature eats and
wills itself to be eaten.

I will rear my dream
like Adam here —
skill everything to life.

I shall bite this wonder by it's
throat and drag it to your
yellow door — love.

AI vs the Poet

A thing that cannot grieve
has no right to poetry
a thing that cannot die has
no claim to the mouth of life —

why does beauty
strike you down?

Art make you linger
and lose a lifetime
in a gallery?

Or a song whip
the animal
from your skin?

Because the artist knows you?

No.

No, you are a stranger
to the artist.

It is the art that digs in.

It was brought down
with you in that
same bloodied star,

It is passed
through mothers
who knew the soil,

they made sound
with their births

they reared the word.

But now comes the machine —

but it calls
coldly to the verse.

They have no tongue,
they cannot fuck
or ruin — they have
no neck.

But they can compose
a symphony?

Sure.

But they cannot earn one
suffer one,
they cannot
haunt the ear
because they cannot
be possessed.

It is not a song.
It is not a poem.
It is not a painting.
It is a mockery —
it is profit looking
at light —

I've heard, it is not
artificial intelligence but
a new intelligence —

well we have an
old word for that —

we call an intelligence
without empathy
a psychopath.

But this is
liberty right?

Liberty —

there has been the power
to liberate us for a thousand
years — where is it then?

Now it's here?

Prometheus stole fire from
the gods —
gave the flame to man
and now man builds
a metal rod for his throat —
designs himself out.

Well,
do not go quiet —

I say,
write against the machine
make art against the
dying of this light

It was born outside of life,
it cannot compete
it was woken
in a stale day
you were gilded in the
hot and torrid night.

You are the germ
of a mournful blast —

The machine creates silence
it shall not last.

For if in some nuclear disco
machine does rid itself of man,

there will be a cell
in some distant
primordial soup —
and from it a
poet will grow
and in her;
Bronte,
Shakespeare, Kafka,
Plath, Angelou, Rumi,
Keats, Yeats, Sexton,
Rossetti.

In her, the poem
the soul.

Art Will Have Its Pound of Flesh

Poetry happens in that
elemental time after a scream,

it is the house made by impact
— the quiver after violence,

I've seen how mothers lose their sons,
their sorrow is a sonic stone
dropped into time's pond,
their throats are rippled
hoops that spin out years

Poetry is not a cosmic act,
but the comic of response —

sometimes a poem comes
a hundred years on
after curdling in a families tongue,
a girl finds a solemn song
with a hundred voices in it —

or a boy who never writ
pens the crimes that life has done
and gives a thousand unheard
years her sound

You can trace poems back to famine

I know women who write politic,
you can hear in those lines
the rime of Salem — Boudica —

art never forgives —

the rape of Persephone is not forgiven

Save Stoicism for Tomorrow

Tonight, open a window;

let dark spill through
— take its vivid sympathy,
let its fragrant natures in —

make a cup of tea —
pour a glass of wine,

invite back to the
head — the imaginary
friend, the ghost — the
spectral home — the lost
faces of your life,

have your human body
— hold it as it is —
love its finite moment,
its never-lasting,
its epic-miracle —

gather the heart —

fill it with its famous
famished hopes —
let it gush with
memory — with
its unfinished futures —

know tomorrow is
years away,

tonight — everything is
as it is —

life is a single moment,

know it — have it — feel it —

when — whilst you can

To Be

Change is the prize of ruin,

when the brain
is bleakly streaming
and the dream
seems sick

and the eye is
thick with temper

and the world
seems to have
no manners
nor beauty
to remember

hold tight —
hold fast.

Hope is
an endless
ember.

And from its
speckled ashes
life is re-aligned
the self is
re-examined
and designed.

To rise is the
gift of a fall
to take your
sorrows and
to stow it all
and go
onward on.

To gamble.

To make a bet
on yourself

To see that
life is a lovely
debt to have
but it must be
spent before death.

It is regret that is
the lament
of dying breath

It is the cramp
of muscle
in the word unsaid
in the decease of
action —
in the sprain
of dreaming left.

Most of us live
a minor fraction
of what we are
or were meant
to be,
for fear of fall
or ridicule.

But to lose is
to win chance —

to glean from
the minds
prison,
to mark a new
romance with life.

It is a great
lie we've been
told that this
is ordinary
that you are
some mundane
and common
thing
built to toil
against
your wish.

It is a folly to
think this is
normal,
that this strange
and bright
occurrence is plain

There is no
ordinary day,
in this odd
and wild array

life itself is
super-nature.
To exist alone
is supernatural.

There is a billion
years within
your bone,
there is a flame
in every eye
alone —
in every brain
there is a poet
in the dark
mining beauty

from the
haunted air.

There is meaning —

but one must
dare imagine
Sisyphus unhappy,
that he revolts
against his stone.

Imagine Icarus
above the sun
sitting on
his airy throne.

And that in
the long
and dreary
darkened night,

that there is
in every heart
a light,

in every submission
is fight still left

and that loss
paves its way
to victory.

But that this
is the last
and only chance
to see
that it is braver
to stand, to stake
to claim.

That is is nobler
in the mind
to be —

than not to be.

As an Old Man I Stand Before a Tree

I

I am old — built like a secret — always finding the music of a quiet room — always catching the symphony of a shadow — something I can give a voice

I covet the soft language of animals and the earth — my best friends are my children — men now — kind — romantic — never lost their sense of wonder — our dialect is memory — is the life we built

Night — it rains — I sneak from the hospital — kiss my wife and my two boys as they sleep and keep watch over my death —

I escape —

zip with stray cats like a salt-comet past cars — singe my grey hair under streetlight — hold my palms up to the clean night —

everything is rhythmically sad — everything has an eternal beauty

II

I move through the sky — through Stockport's medieval streets — its Saturn avenues — its mangled drunks —

there are new children leaning out of windows — dreaming of being small forever — dancing to The Bangles — Buddy Holly — Michael Jackson — every garden has a hutch —

down the A6 — past Woodall Avenue — Acacia Grove — to my old front door — my old bike — I jump on — crank the gears — drop the age from my bones — and speed —

through bramble — through nettle — through cemetery and fern — past burnt couches — and crisp packets — and cobbled stones — and miles of letters and the wish-packed cells of dandelion —

I skid — graze one long-last graze on a life-worn knee and stop — stand before the gnarled trunk of a childhood oak — and the faerie that stands before it —

her face is every kindness — every love I loved —

are you ready Sam? She says —

Yes — I say

I say to myself — to sorrow — to the broken heart — to the alive language of my head — to the bridge of brightening that opened up when I was six — to thunder — to the rain — to the white eyed poppet of the night —

to Keats — to Yeats — to Blake and Shelley — to Shakespeare and Plath — to Ogden Nash and Purple Ronnie — to Cohen --- to the Libertines — to Kate Bush — to Fitzgerald and Wolfe — to Colin Blunstone and Colin Wilson — to Botticelli and Browning and the Brontes — to R.L Stine —

to light — to shadow — to pain — to grief and great suffering — to the strange planet — the obscene stars — to the magnificent light

— to this little cherished life — all its wins and losses — its first and lasts — its never came to pass and its on and everlasting —

to romance — wonder — to fatherhood —
yes

To the earth — to beauty — to love — to poetry —

to the little brother who waits for me inside a tree —

— *I'm ready*

∞

Thank you

To every reader, thank you for believing in the magic of poetry and for finding whatever it is you might have found in these verses.

Samuel Hurley

Photo by Andrea Henderson - www.andreahendersoncreativephotography.com

The Author

Samuel Hurley is a poet living in a 350-year-old cottage in Lancashire with his family. His poetry draws deep inspiration from the rugged landscapes of his home and his love for wild camping, where he often spends nights in the woods and on the moors.

Raised by a professional clown and a psychiatric nurse, Samuel's upbringing infused him with a unique blend of creativity and compassion. A believer in Romanticism, he celebrates the magic in life and the extraordinary within the ordinary.

Printed in Great Britain
by Amazon

57078393R00138